"The Psalms are for every r sorrow, every anxiety, and e .... y, a wise and loving pastor illustrates and applies the biblical psalms in ways that help everyday Christians connect the gospel to the ups and downs of everyday life."

Philip G. Ryken, President, Wheaton College; council member of the Alliance of Confessing Evangelicals; author of more than thirty books

"*Soul Anatomy* by my friend Pastor George Robertson is both personally honest and pastorally helpful. His honesty and vulnerability make me think, 'Oh, I'm not alone.' His help and wisdom make me think, 'Oh, Jesus is real—right where I need him.' This book gently puts the hand of the reader into the hand of Christ our Healer. Who doesn't need that?"

Ray Ortlund, Renewal Ministries, Nashville, TN

"Dr. George Robertson is a rarity among today's theologians; a scholar with a common touch. In these psalms, Dr. Robertson combines scholarly precision with everyday living. You will come away from reading these words feeling that you have been to a banquet of grace—you have—and will look forward to coming back for more. Your life will be uplifted and your soul renewed by the spiritual feast found on these pages. I cannot recommend them too highly."

Leslie Holmes, Former Provost, Erskine Theological Seminary

"In *Soul Anatomy*, George Robertson has combined insightful and engaging exegesis of God's songbook (The Psalms) with practical, helpful, and personal applications of these eternal truths. This book will be treasured by anyone who desires a more intimate relationship with their Creator and Redeemer."

Paul Kooistra, Former President, Erskine College

"All too often, Christians aren't sure how to deal with the ebb and flow of their emotions, with the challenge of their circumstances, or with the painful reality of opposition. Yet God has given us an entire book of the Bible that serves as 'an anatomy of the soul'—the Psalms. I can't think of a better guide through this God-given book of counsel and help than Dr. George Robertson."

Sean Michael Lucas, Senior Minister, Independent Presbyterian Church, Memphis, TN

"George Robertson has not only mined the Psalms for the theological truths that apply the gospel 'oil upon the troubled waters' of both heart and soul but has done so with a pastor's touch. Enjoy the gospel melody from Christ, the Singer of the Psalms, as he refreshes your heart and soul on every page of this faithful and insightful volume."

Harry L. Reeder, III, Senior Pastor,
Briarwood Presbyterian Church, Birmingham, AL

"George Robertson's work in *Soul Anatomy* is latent with the effects of years served in faithful and fruitful pastoral ministry. The human heart is expressed so emotively in the psalms, and this exposition is enlightened by the experience of a pastor who has cared for many through all ranges of the lived experience."

Stephen Um, Senior Minister,
Citylife Presbyterian Church, Boston, MA

"Robertson's work brings out the full intention of the Psalms to meet head-on the emotional states of the heart common to us all. There is nary a human feeling that the Psalms do not address. One will particularly appreciate this pastor/scholar's good use of illustrations, both personal and historical, that center on feelings of apprehension, rest, despair, and elation. This author's writing is comprehensive and reads well for pastors, counselors, and laymen alike."

Robert Vasholz, Professor Emeritus,
Covenant Theological Seminary, St. Louis, MO

"Only now am I appreciating the riches and depth of the Psalms for our spiritual nurture and growth, and Pastor Robertson's book is a welcome aid in this exploration. His mediations on these divine yet very human words help to heal my wounds and lift my soul. I recommend this volume to all who want to be nourished by our Lord's prayer book."

Bill Kynes, Pastor,
Cornerstone Evangelical Free Church, Annandale, VA

"To be honest, I'm not the emotive type, and the soul-stirring beauty of the Psalms has often eluded me. Thus, it was a great day to discover that George Robertson—a scholar, devoted shepherd of his flock, and prince among preachers—was publishing his work on the Psalms. For strugglers like me, *Soul Anatomy* is medicine my parched heart craves."

Ray Cortese, Senior Pastor,
Seven Rivers Presbyterian Church, Lecanto, FL

Soul Anatomy

Finding Peace, Hope, and Joy
in the Psalms

George Robertson

New
Growth
Press

WWW.NEWGROWTHPRESS.COM

New Growth Press, Greensboro, NC 27404
newgrowthpress.com

Cover Design: Faceout Books, faceoutstudios.com
Interior Design and Typesetting: Gretchen Logterman

ISBN: 978-1-64507-038-2 (Print)
ISBN: 978-1-64507-039-9 (eBook)

Library of Congress Control Number: 2020933310

Printed in Canada

27 26 25 24 23 22 21 20   1 2 3 4 5

To Jackie

You are truly a Christiana
as Alexander Whyte described her:

"Her heart, her deep, strong, tender heart, is present on
every page of Christiana's noble history. Her heart keeps
her often silent when the water in her eyes becomes all
the more eloquent. . . But it was not so much what she
said herself that brought out the depth and tenderness
of Christiana's heart, it was rather the way her heart
loosened other people's tongues. . . Christiana did
not speak much to her guides and instructors and
companions, but they always spoke their best to her,
and it was her heart that did it."
—Bunyan Characters in the *Pilgrim's Progress*

Any good speech in the following pages
has been inspired by you.

And to

Taylor, Anna, Abbey, and Caroline

You are the greatest blessings of our lives.
Psalm 128:3

Contents

Acknowledgements

we had moved to STL + joined Covenant!

I PREACHED ON Psalm 1 for the first time on September 24, 1998. From there I figured I would preach only on my favorites or those more familiar. Maybe I would lead my congregation through fifty or so? But once I started, I couldn't skip any! On November 18, 2001, I preached on Psalm 150 after writing sermons on every psalm in between, including ten on Psalm 119. At my next call, over the course of five years of Sunday evening services, I preached again through all 150. Preaching through the Psalter one more time before I die is on my bucket list. The point is, I can't get enough of the Psalms. I've discovered through these two preaching experiences that the same is true for most Christians. One of the greatest blessings has been the conversations and letters. After each sermon, at least one person has shared a past experience in which that text had become "their psalm." Augustine said the Scriptures "find us." This is especially true of the Psalter. They find us wherever we are spiritually, emotionally, physically. Regardless of how my life is going, I can spend time in the Psalms and the psalmist puts his arm around me and says, "I have walked this same road, and this is what I have discovered about God and myself." After studying the Psalms over the last twenty years, I realize this fellow pilgrim is not just "a psalmist," it is Jesus, the Good Shepherd. May you meet him more intimately than ever as you slow down and tarry over the Psalms in this volume.

This same Good Shepherd has used many people to bring this book into being. I am deeply indebted to my first "favorite people" at The Covenant Presbyterian of St. Louis. This noble congregation dared to call me as their pastor when I was only twenty-three years old. As my twenty-five-year-old son exclaimed recently, "What were they thinking?!" They watched me grow up and patiently encouraged me over the fifteen years I was there. Our tour through the Psalms was an exciting adventure. Rhonda Sarafolean, Charlotte McLaughlin, and Lois Miller were the faithful assistants who managed my complicated professional life while also running down resources and editing manuscripts. Then my beloved congregation at First Presbyterian in Augusta also made it possible to focus most of my energy on crafting sermons, including revising these on the Psalms. Vonnie Eidson, my Executive Assistant, spent many hours editing, reformatting, and promoting this concept to publishers. After receiving several rejections from publishers who said the "Psalms don't sell," we put away the idea and focused our energies on other things. However, Vonnie always believed other people needed to hear what the Lord had taught two congregations. During those fallow years, my Old Testament professor, mentor, and friend, Dr. Robert I. Vasholz, edited every sermon for exegetical accuracy. His only requested remuneration was time off to go to Israel and for me to purchase *for him* Mitchell Dahood's three-volume commentary in the Anchor series. That I went with him to Israel and the commentaries are on my shelf, not his, reflect the generosity I have always known from him. Around 2015, one of my seminary students, Josh Preston, asked to take a crack at creating a smaller collection of the sermons for publication. After moving to Memphis to serve as my research assistant at Second Presbyterian, Josh put his shoulder to the work transforming the studies from sermons into book chapters and securing a publisher. If not for Josh and my Executive Assistant, Amanda Coop (the "Dream Team"), this book would have never been finished. They are consummate professionals, savvy businesspersons, skilled wordsmiths, overly generous cheerleaders, and life-giving friends. Josh is supernaturally gifted as a writer, editor, teacher, and pastor. His labors over this manuscript almost make it more his than mine. Amanda's dramatic personality keeps us all laughing while she manages my life (and my family's, too) providing the margin I need to think, pray, study, prepare, lead, and preach.

While my officers, staff, and congregation at Second Presbyterian have not heard these sermons in full, I would not be able to preach and write with the joy and devotion I do without their loving support. My dear people at Second Presbyterian weekly astound me with their eagerness to respond to the grace of God in the same way the psalmists did. With the sons of Korah, I remember "how I go with the throng and lead them in processions to the house of God with glad shouts and songs of praise, a multitude keeping festival" (Psalm 42:4).

My most helpful critics are my children Taylor, Anna, Abbey, and Caroline. Each one is a student of God's word and has impossibly high standards for preaching. Their insights, prodding, affirmation, and the beauty of their lives provide constant inspiration. Apart from the Holy Spirit, no one deserves more credit for whatever the Lord has done in my ministry than my wife Jackie. I preach the gospel, but she lives it. She is my north star, the truest standard of unconditional love in my life. She loves and lives the Psalms. My only nervousness about Jackie is how much she loves the imprecatory psalms! Her familiarity with them provides strong inspiration for me to stay on her good side. Jackie stubbornly loves me through all the vicissitudes of my emotional life and thus incarnates to me the One who walks with me even in the valley of the shadow.

Finally, I must thank New Growth Press for believing in this book. It has been the privilege of a lifetime to work with their extraordinary staff. Their standards are dauntingly high, reflecting their commitment to minister the grace of Jesus excellently to their readers. Barbara Juliani and Ruth Castle have made me a much better writer as well as a better pastor.

Soli Deo Gloria

George W. Robertson
Memphis, Tennessee
December 2019

Introduction

In your light do we see light.
(Psalm 36:9)

"I LOVE THE Psalms!" I cannot begin to guess how many times in my thirty years of ministry I've heard someone make that declaration. I don't remember hearing anyone exclaim, "I just love the book of Numbers!" Many have told me that Romans revolutionized their doctrine of God, or that Galatians set them free from legalism. However, I've gotten the strong impression that if those I've had the privilege of pastoring were forced to pick just one book in the Bible they could have on a desert island, it would be the book of Psalms.

This is true for me as a preacher: Psalms is one of my favorite texts to preach. This is even more true for me as a Christian. For most of my life I have battled anxiety and depression, so I have lived more in the Psalms than any other place in the Bible. When my heart is breaking, when my soul is anxious, when my mind is troubled, when my faith burns low, when my hope for the future is obscured, when I'm angry at God's providence, I find comfort in the Psalms.

In this volume I have collected the psalms I return to most often when I particularly need *peace, hope,* and *joy.* Those who have anxious spirits like mine understand when I say the night can be dreadful. When we can't distract ourselves with activity and the normal hustle-and-bustle noises of the daytime fade away, we are left with our thoughts. I have found no better sleeping aid than a promise of peace, hope, joy—or usually all three—from one of these twenty-five psalms.

The Psalms were written thousands of years ago. Most literature doesn't survive more than a few hundred years. What explains their enduring power? Here are five reasons—and I'm sure there are many more.

Psalm 36:9 clearly describes the first reason: "For with you is the fountain of life; in your light do we see light." The Psalms invite us to understand ourselves—in all our ups and downs—in the light of God's true reality. Second, the Psalms increase our boldness in prayer, a discipline every Christian is weak in. John Calvin said, "[The Psalms] have opened up to us familiar access to God."[1] Third, they give voice to our deepest griefs and show us a way to rightly process our suffering. Fourth, as poetic expressions of the faith, they ground us in life-changing theology. They are not dry doctrinal statements; they teach us truths about God through poems that appeal to our senses and connect us with our deepest emotional experiences. The poets who wrote the Psalms knew redemptive history and interpreted their circumstances in light of it. Fifth, they grow us in community; they show the church how to live together and how to care for one another.

The Psalms were part of the ordinary weekly worship of Israel. Sadness, happiness, victory, defeat, sin, redemption, judgment, anger, and mourning all came to expression with the help of the Psalter. We study the Psalms in order to respond to God, just like the psalmists did. One of the ways we do that is by speaking the language of the Psalms until they become our faith—the early church referred to this as *lex orandi, lex credendi* ("law of praying, law of believing"). Training our brains, moving our tongues, focusing our hearts, and bending our bodies the way the psalmists call us to do will shape our souls. As divinely inspired

2

prayers, God is providing vocabulary that he welcomes from us when we do not know how to pray.

C. S. Lewis observed, "[T]he Psalms are poems, and poems are intended to be sung: not doctrinal treatises, nor even sermons."[2] But how do you sing when you're anxious? How do you worship when you're depressed? Where do you find words to express inexpressible joy? What do you pray when you need to rest?

As you read the Psalms from beginning to end, you will find a God-authored script by which the full gamut of human experience can be expressed. John Calvin referred to the Psalter as "an anatomy of all parts of the soul."[3] The Bible's inspired hymnbook guides the believer through the highest summits and lowest valleys of life, and invites the not-yet believer to a Redeemer who, as a "man of sorrows" (Isaiah 53:3), experienced fully the emotions of these prayers. Since the Psalms are ultimately the prayers of Jesus, their full expression of human emotion convinces us that Jesus really is a high priest who can sympathize with us (Hebrews 4:15). As you read this book, I hope you will develop a vocabulary to express your own experiences and see Jesus more clearly.

The best way for you to read each chapter will be to read the psalm first. Most of the subheadings in each chapter contain references for the specific verses being referred to. This will enable you to go back and see exactly where in the psalm these concepts come from and how the psalmist, and ultimately Jesus, dealt with the various issues raised throughout the Psalter.

1

The Truly Happy Person

Psalm 1

For the LORD watches over the way of the righteous.
(Psalm 1:6, NIV)

THIS IS A book about two ways. Many of us know the one way all too well—the way that leads away from God. Naturally we all go our own way, but this psalm is calling us to a better way—following God and living a blessed life with him. This way is the one Jesus marks out for us and promises to travel with us. On this way with Jesus we can (and will) still experience moments of anxiety, depression, or despair. I battle anxiety and depression daily! At a few points in my life, I have been on the brink of despair. But walking with Jesus and going God's way means we possess peace, hope, and joy, which are ultimately more powerful than anxiety, depression, and despair. Jesus promised we would have troubles in this world (John 16:33). The greatest figures in redemptive history from Moses to David to Paul have battled despair. Some of the greatest leaders in church history from Augustine to Calvin to Spurgeon had crippling seasons of anxiety and depression. These sometimes terrifying emotions are not disqualifications for believers. On the contrary, we discover in the Psalms a Savior whose love is so powerful that it keeps us praying with resilient hope *while* the feelings persist.

The Psalms are the inspired hymnbook for the pilgrim following the eternally fulfilling way of Jesus. Jesus is the trailblazer for that narrow path, and the Psalms provide a record of his emotional journey. They prove that Jesus becoming like us in every way included experiencing the emotions all humans experience. But Jesus also showed us how to translate our emotions into prayers to the Father.

As a new believer, Psalm 1 was the first passage of Scripture I memorized; and I have been returning to it ever since. When life gets confusing or overwhelming, returning to this psalm helps renew my perspective. There is only one way that brings peace, hope, and joy, and that way is marked out by Jesus. I need to close my ears to all competing agendas for my life and ask myself, "Where does Jesus want to lead me?"

Allow me to place your hand in Jesus's, and allow him to walk you across the threshold of Psalm 1 into the Psalter—and, I pray, into a lifetime of walking and praying with Jesus.

Once, while getting to know a new Christian, I asked several questions about his life. For a young man, he had an incredibly diverse life, full of intriguing experiences. When he finished recounting one particularly fascinating story, I said, "You have had a very interesting life." "Interesting, yes," he responded, "but fulfilling and happy, no." He then went on to say that only recently had his life become fulfilling and joyful, because he had received Christ and was finally living the way God had designed.

Is that true of you? Are you trying to face the anxieties of life in God's way and with his resources, or in your way with limited perspective and inadequate resources?

Psalm 1 contains a promise and a warning. It promises that living according to God's will, even while encountering all the same trials as unbelievers, is accompanied by profoundly deeper peace, hope, and joy. Conversely, it warns that living any other way results in hopelessness, purposelessness, and ultimate destruction. The psalmist emphasizes this point by describing each way of life and contrasting the two ways.

The Way of Blessing (vv. 1–3)

The psalmist does not leave us guessing about which is the better way. He paints two contrasting portraits vividly displaying the difference between those who try to walk in their own strength and own wisdom through a broken world and those who walk through the same broken world relying on the Lord.

Avoids evil influence (v. 1)

Right from the beginning we are faced with a choice: avoid evil or embrace it. The person who follows God avoids the influence of evil. Notice in verse 1 the gradual slope that involvement in evil can take.

"Walks." Going toward evil can begin by simply "walking in the counsel of the wicked," paying heed to their advice. We can easily think like the rest of the world and take our cues for life not from God but from those around us. Perhaps we justify it by saying, "After all, all truth is God's truth. This sounds like truth to me, so I will follow it this time."

By the way, the word "wicked" (resha`im) could be literally translated "those who are loose." In other words, the wicked are loose from God; they get into trouble. Consequently their advice is loose from God and prescribes trouble for those who follow it.

"Stands." The next step after following the advice of the wicked is to stand in their way—to linger at their door in such a way that one now becomes a party to their evil. The word translated "sinner" is chatta'im, meaning "missing the mark." These people plot how they might do that which misses God's mark of holiness.

"Sits." If he does not walk away, the final step is to sit down and congregate with "scoffers." This is the most frightening level, because a scoffer is one who actually mocks holiness and God's ways. This is the farthest one can get from repentance. The person who began by listening to the advice of wicked people, went on to linger at their door, and then plotted sin with them has now become a full-fledged member of their scoffing company.

Absorbs God's Word (v. 2)

Notice that this person is not just characterized by what he does not do, but by what he pursues. As we study the Psalms, we will notice that Hebrew poetry is often composed of parallelisms—the same idea is said in two different ways or with two different images. That enriches our understanding. Verse 2 is a good example of parallelism. In the first half of the verse, the psalmist concludes a thought started in verse 1: "Blessed is the one . . . whose delight is in the law of the Lord" (NIV). The second half of verse 2 tells us specifically how he does so: "he meditates on it day and night" (HCSB). In other words, your delight is not in simply speaking about the Bible, but rather by ruminating over it, reading, and rereading, so that it becomes a part of your life.

You may have noticed that I take "the law of the Lord" to mean the Bible. Is it accurate to say that the psalmist delights in the whole Bible, or just the Ten Commandments? The word *torah* will come up many times in our study of the Psalms. It will be important each time to determine whether it refers to the whole of the Scriptures or purely to "the law of the Lord." More often than not, it will refer to the whole Bible. We know this from verses like Joshua 1:7, in which *torah* refers to "all the law" of Moses's writings, not just the Ten Commandments; from 2 Kings 17:13, where *torah* refers to the writings "delivered . . . through . . . the prophets" (NIV); and from John 15:25, where Jesus quotes Psalms 35:19 and 69:4, referring to them as the "Law." That is also the case in Psalm 1:2. The happy person will be the one who sets aside time to read, reread, and ponder Scripture and its application to her life.

If you are battling anxiety, depression, or despair right now, you may be frustrated with these explanations. "Why do I need to know about parallelism or the *torah*? I'm drowning in my fears!" But it turns out that God knows how to speak to an anxious soul. When we are anxious it's hard to concentrate. It's hard to hear and remember God's words to us, so God helps us by using parallelisms to repeat things. He has lots of different ways to say: "I am here. I am with you. I am not going to leave you. I am by your side." God repeats himself not merely for poetic flourish, but because he knows how to attend to worried souls who have trouble hearing comforting truth above the cacophony of their fears.

Even when God calls you to do something (law) it is because he loves you and wants life to go well with you. Most importantly, he gave his only Son to die for your sins, so you can always be assured that he will forgive you and help you turn to him and his way. A Reformer used to say, "There is no law-music in heaven."[1] Well, neither is there law-music in Scripture. It is all grace. It is all gospel. In your most despairing moments, you can turn to Scripture and hear a gracious God speaking to you. The psalms are especially rich with comfort from your heavenly Father, who knows how to reassure a soul deafened by fear.

Achieves their purpose in life (v. 3)

Notice how the life of one who avoids evil and absorbs God's Word is characterized: "That person is like a tree planted by streams of water, which yields its fruit in season and whose leaf does not wither—whatever they do prospers" (v. 3, NIV). The long-term effect will be a life that achieves its purpose. Isn't that what we all want? Here is the promise to you: when you are well nourished by God's Word ("streams of water"), God produces through you good works ("fruit") that are appropriate to your stage in life ("in season"), relevant, needed by the world you live in at the time ("leaf does not wither"), and eternally prosperous.

This has meaningful implications, especially for our work. Perhaps you are disillusioned with your current work situation because it is not something you enjoy. Or maybe it is something you enjoy but you do not feel you are getting the opportunity to do really important and exciting work. Perhaps your work involves caring for your children each day, and the daily routine feels monotonous at times. The promise of this psalm is that those who root themselves in God will produce "fruit in season." We need only be concerned with pursuing God's will; the fruit we produce in each season of life will be exactly the fruit he has planned for us.

The Way of Irrelevance (vv. 4–5)

The way of blessing is starkly contrasted by the way of irrelevance in verses 4–5. What is true of those who follow any other way besides walking by faith? The image is horrifying because it is the way of irrelevance.

Chaff

The first way the psalmist describes the wicked is as "chaff" (v. 4). In the psalmist's day, farmers would take the grain they had harvested to an elevated threshing floor. There they would dump everything: straw, stubble, chaff, grain. They would then throw everything in the air with their hands or pitchfork. The grain, being heavier, would fall back to the threshing floor, but the chaff, light and worthless, would be carried away by the wind.

Here the psalmist says that the lives of the wicked will blow away. They will not accomplish anything of eternal significance. Their most important accomplishments will still be time bound and subject to decay.

Judgment

The picture continues to get worse. The psalmist says not only that their lives will amount to nothing of true significance, but that they "will not stand in the judgment" (v. 5). Though they may stand with great pomp in the way of sinners, they will not survive

God's judgment, which will destroy their works and forever consume them (Mark 9:43, 48).

This passage reminds us of a parable Jesus told in Matthew 13:24–30. The farmer, representing Christ, sowed good seeds (Christians) in his field (the world). But an enemy (the devil) sowed weeds (his followers) in with the good seed. But the wise farmer was not too disturbed. He would let them grow up together until the time of the harvest. When the wheat formed heads, it would be obvious which was wheat and which was weed. The servants would pull up the weeds first, gather them in a pile, and burn them. Then they could clearly see to harvest the grain.

The true children of God will be revealed by good works that are performed out of a heart made new by Jesus Christ. The weeds will be revealed by works that are done outside of a relationship to Christ. The root of those weeds is a heart that is going its own way, not God's way. This person is self-centered and cannot love God and others. The result is a life that, in the end, is blown away.

The Disparity of the Ways (v. 6)

The psalmist continues his descriptions of the two ways, so as to impress upon us the vanity of our self-conceived way with inadequate resources for an anxiety-ridden world and the grace of God's way with bottomless stores of peace, hope, and joy for moments of anxiety, depression, or despair.

Lost

The way of the wicked—these loose ones, having no weight, no significance, and no bearing—is to drift through life feeling that one is the subject of a capricious Mother Nature, "the Force," or nothing at all. The end of that way is destruction. H. G. Wells described the end for the wicked when he said: "Man who began in a cave behind a windbreak will end in the diseased soaked ruins of a slum."[2]

Known

But how different is God's way! He watches over the righteous. He is "our refuge and strength, an ever-present help in trouble" (Psalm 46:1, NIV); "He will cover you with his feathers, and under his wings you will find refuge" (Psalm 91:4, NIV); "He will not let your foot slip—he who watches over you will not slumber. . . . The LORD watches over you—the LORD is your shade at your right hand; the sun will not harm you by day, nor the moon by night. The LORD will keep you from all harm—he will watch over your life; the LORD will watch over your coming and going both now and forevermore" (Psalm 121:3, 5–8).

Are you discouraged by these contrasting images of the way of blessing and irrelevance? Each of us desires happiness, but we are also well aware of the ways we fail to imitate this truly blessed person described in Psalm 1. It is imperative, then, that we understand what this psalm— and all of the Psalms, for that matter—is truly about.

The Bible teacher Joseph Flacks once visited the Middle East and had the opportunity to address a gathering of Jews and Arabs. After reading Psalm 1, he asked, "Who is this blessed man of whom the psalmist speaks? This man never walked in the counsel of the wicked or stood in the way of sinners or sat in the seat of mockers. He was an absolutely sinless man."

Nobody spoke, so Flacks asked: "Was he our great father Abraham?"

One elderly man said, "No, it cannot be Abraham. He denied his wife and told a lie about her."

"Well, how about the lawgiver Moses?" Flacks asked again.

"No," someone said. "It cannot be Moses. He killed a man, and he lost his temper by the waters of Meribah."

Flacks then suggested David. But it could not be the adulterer and murderer David either.

There was silence for a long while. Then an elderly Jew arose and said, "My brothers, I have a little book here; it is called the New Testament. I have been reading it; and if I could believe this book, if I could be sure that it is true, I would say that the man of the first Psalm was Jesus of Nazareth."[3]

This man was absolutely right. Jesus is the blessed man of Psalm 1. Jesus Christ leads us through these psalms to understand more of him; to lead us on the right way. He is the truly blessed man who perfectly avoided evil for our sake, who perfectly appropriated the Word of God for our sake, and who died on the tree to produce fruit in us and make us people who stand on the day of judgment because Jesus did it all and paid it all. Because he made peace with God through the cross, he is our peace. Because he secured the hope of the glory of God, he is our hope. And because he went to the cross in joy, he is our joy. The truly peaceful, hopeful, and joyful person is the one who follows Jesus who is *the* Way.

Questions for Reflection/Discussion

1. What resonated with you most from this chapter?

2. How does understanding that Jesus is the truly blessed man sharpen your focus when you read the Psalms?

3. What does this mean for your own pursuit of hope, peace, and joy?

Prayer

As divinely inspired prayers, the Psalms are wonderful guides for our own conversations with God. Slowly read through each section of Psalm 1, stopping to pray the Psalm in your own words and considering how to apply each section to your own life. Here is one way to approach it:

- Thank God that his Word is a sturdy foundation for you, providing peace for your heart and mind in good times and bad (v. 2).
- Ask God to help you delight in his promises and to become the kind of person who meditates on them consistently (v. 2).
- Thank God that in the middle of difficult times, you can rest in the promise that he will accomplish his work in your heart and life (v. 3).
- Pray for a deeper commitment to those in your community of faith, thanking God for how he uses the body of Christ to sharpen you and keep you on the path of life (vv. 1, 5).

2

I Know His Hands

Psalm 5

Give ear to my words, O Lord; consider my groaning.
(Psalm 5:1)

IN PSALM 1 we introduced the idea that peace, hope, and joy come from Jesus walking with us. Psalm 5 takes it a step further, assuring us that he not only walks with us but pays careful attention to us. The Bible consistently assures us that God loves to pay attention to us. God's delight in paying attention to us is not something we naturally believe, so he reminds us often. And because we are also not naturally inclined to believe that his grace is available to all who humbly ask, we must be trained and retrained in the art of asking.

This is one of the reasons there are so many psalms. As a large collection of prayers, the Psalms show us how belief in a gracious, attentive Savior transforms the way we call out to God in our troubles. Knowing that God pays attention to every detail of our lives and cares about all our concerns encourages us to go to him with everything. The psalmists teach us how to take everything in our hearts to the Lord—our joys, our gratitude, our worries, our troubles. We never have to wait until our hearts are "acceptable" before we go to him; we go to him in whatever condition our hearts are in, so he might unburden them. The King of the universe is ever present with us regardless of what we are going through. Prayer is that means of grace by which we remain mindful that we are connected to a sovereign Shepherd.

One of the greatest hymns on prayer issues this invitation: "Come, My Soul, Thy Suit Prepare." As a kid, one of my friends thought the hymn was about getting your clothes ready for church! But John Newton, the hymnist, was actually conveying Jesus's eagerness to answer our prayers. In Puritan fashion, Newton urges us to lay out our need before a righteous Judge who will always rule in our favor, because his Son advocates for us, making our case to the Father:

> Jesus loves to answer prayer
> He himself has bid thee pray,
> Therefore will not say thee nay.[1]

One reason we find it difficult to pray is that we don't believe that God cares about our needs. Perhaps some needs seem too small ("Help me find a parking place"), while other needs seem too large ("Heal my child from cancer"). But God cares about everything you care about and wants to hear your groanings. We don't need to rescue ourselves; we have a Rescuer. Do you think your need is too great for him? It is not. God is all-powerful and all-loving. The psalmist, King David, goes to God because he understands God's fatherly character: God is attentive, merciful, and just. His character is our invitation to prayer.

Attentive (vv. 1–3)

When my son Taylor turned four, I arranged a unique surprise birthday party. He and his friends went for a ride on a 1929 REO fire truck. What made the ride particularly meaningful to me was the man who drove it: the owner of the truck and my neighbor, "Mr. Charley." Most of our neighbors were afraid of Mr. Charley. He looked like a mean old curmudgeon, but he was actually a very gracious man who became my friend. When my neighbors heard that he provided the fire truck, they were incredulous, "How did you ever work up the courage to ask him?" I simply responded, "It didn't require courage; he's a friend."

Perhaps due to certain experiences, teaching, or the example of others, you imagine God to be unapproachable, even angry. Understanding that God is in fact attentive when we pray will change the way and the frequency with which we pray.

Knowing the Father to be the God of peace, hope, and joy compels us to run to him without hesitation. Earlier I said Christ is our *advocate*. Because this is true, we can be especially bold in going immediately to the Father. An advocate takes up someone else's cause. A lawyer advocates for her client to a judge. A guardian ad litem advocates for the rights of a neglected child. A lobbyist advocates for lawmakers for legislation favorable to industry. Jesus advocates for his people. But he does not wait until we pray to do so. The Bible says, "we *have* an advocate with the Father, Jesus Christ the righteous" (1 John 2:1, emphasis added). One of my fellow pastors often says, "Let's now join Jesus who is already at prayer for us." Whenever we pray, we can remember that Jesus has already been praying and advocating for us. Charles Wesley encourages us to be bold in all our prayers by remembering,

> Five bleeding wounds he bears
> Received on Calvary.
> They pour effectual prayers.
> They kindly plead for me.[2]

Our gracious and friendly God eagerly responds to all kinds of requests (vv. 1–3). He listens to our "words" (v. 1), even carefully composed, thoughtful petitions. David also knows that God listens to "lament[s]" (v. 1, NIV), sighing, deep, inarticulate prayers that we express when we are unable to speak words. God also attends to cries (v. 2)—desperate, immediate pleas in the midst of distress.

What an amazing thing that God hears us at all, much less gives attention to our unspoken prayers. Isn't it amazing that he actually discerns the silent cries of our hearts? One of the great lines of the Bible occurs when Abraham sent Hagar and Ishmael away because Sarah despised her concubine's son (Genesis 21:9). When Hagar had run out of provisions, she set Ishmael under a bush in the desert because she could not bear to watch him starve to death. Then the Bible says, "God heard the boy crying" (Genesis 21:17, NIV). The God who upholds the universe molecule by molecule, who is actively waging war with his cosmic enemies, who is governing nations and kingdoms, turned his head when a boy cried under a desert bush in the land of Palestine. If God noticed a child's undirected cry, how much more will he listen to the petitions of his children (cf. Luke 18:7–8)?

In verse 2, David uses one of his favorite combination titles for God: "my King and my God" (cf. Psalm 44:4; 68:24; 84:3). Each time David uses this title, he is remembering an aspect of who God is that provides shelter from an assault. Charles Spurgeon often said that the sweetness of the Christian life is found in the personal pronouns of Scripture.[3] David does not merely appeal to *a* God who is *a* king; he appeals to a personally gracious God whom he familiarly addresses as "*my* King and *my* God" (emphasis added). Through this language, David reminded himself that it was not an abstract, distant deity to whom he looked for help but to *his* God. The second stanza of Newton's hymn quoted above goes like this:

> Thou art coming to a King
> Large petitions with thee bring;
> For his grace and pow'r are such,
> None can ever ask too much.

Of course, when we cry to *our* God, we must wait with expectation for God to answer. But as we wait, we should remember who it is that we are praying to, as David does. When we know God's character, we are encouraged to believe that he will answer, no matter how long we may have to wait.

One remarkable story illustrates how we may never know the deep, life-changing effects of persistent and faithful prayer. On January 16, 1998, Sister Mary Paul of the Convent of the Good Shepherd in Liverpool, England, wrote the following letter to the famous journalist Malcolm Muggeridge, whose conversion to Jesus Christ gained the world's attention:

> Dear Mr. Muggeridge,
> Forty-three years ago, in Cairo, a young nun read an article in a journal or newspaper which had been sent out to her from home. She sensed that the writer, a young journalist, was rather confused spiritually and she made up her mind that she would pray for him. Every day of that forty-three years the young man's name was mentioned in prayer, and last week after viewing "Panorama" that same sister, now retired from the mission, turned to me and said, "This is what I have been waiting forty-three years for." The name of the young man—now elderly—was Malcolm Muggeridge and the remark on "Panorama" which sister was referring to was ". . . as a confirmed Christian. . . ." Sister doesn't know that I am telling you this, but, receiving criticism as so many public figures must do, I thought it would be rather a change to know that you have been the object of the thoughts and prayers of an unknown nun these many years.[4]

Here was a man whose intellectual objections to Christianity were formidable, a hardened agnostic who seemed impenetrable to the gospel. But this nun brought her petition to her King and was willing to wait and watch him work. You can never ask too much, because there is no need that can be greater than the God to whom you pray.

Merciful (vv. 4–7)

Attending to the cries of people like us requires great mercy on God's part. To help us appreciate the miracle of God's mercy, David vividly describes God's hatred for sin. The wicked "cannot stand in [his] presence," he "hate[s] all who do wrong," and "destroy[s] those who tell lies" (vv. 4–6, NIV).

The justice of God's wrath against sin often strikes us as unfair, as though the punishment does not fit the crime. But let us consider this: the term "wicked" (*rasha*) refers to one who pursues a "lifestyle contrary to the laws of God (Proverbs 17:15; Daniel 12:10)."[5] To that dreadful action God responds with a restraining order. Those who do "wrong" in verse 5 are those who do vain, foolish things. That sounds less serious, but God says he hates them. We might think, "How could telling a few lies be worse than apostasy?" Yet God destroys liars. I think David is making this dramatic point: all sin is intolerable to God, regardless of how we might rank it. As Paul later wrote, "the wages of sin is death" (Romans 6:23).

In view of God's utter holiness, David's boldness is that much more striking, as he says he "can come into [God's] house" (v. 7, NIV). Sounds self-serving, doesn't it? The apostate, the arrogant, the wrongdoer, and the liar are going to be destroyed by God—while David, the adulterer, murderer, and liar, is going to come into God's presence and pray (see 2 Samuel 11–12)! How can we reconcile this? The answer comes in the mercy of God: "But I, *by your great mercy,* will come into your house" (v. 7, NIV1984, emphasis added). When we understand how terrible our sin is before God, we can begin to appreciate how great his mercy is to us. David prophetically saw that God's Son, Jesus, would save "not because of righteous things we had done, but because of his mercy" (Titus 3:5, NIV). The infinite greatness of God's mercy encourages us to come boldly into his presence with all our petitions.

Just (vv. 8–10)

A humble dependence on God's mercy gives us renewed reverence for God's justice toward his and our enemies. Notice that David's immediate prayer after acknowledging God's mercy is to ask, "Lead me, O LORD, in your righteousness" (v. 8). David asks that God's righteousness or justice would be established in him, that he would walk in God's ways. Why? So that life would go better for him? It certainly would, but that is not the reason stated. Instead, he asks that God would make him live righteously, "because of [his] enemies" (v. 8). In other words, if God does not keep David faithful, it will give David's enemies an opportunity to mock God. That is a prayer of love. Our love for Christ is proportional to our realization of God's mercy (cf. Luke 7:47), and the measure of our love for him will determine how concerned we are about our life's impact on his reputation. Our poor testimony could poorly represent our beloved Savior, which should cause us to pray that it would never happen.

Such loving zeal for Christ's name drives David to pray against God's enemies, saying, "Declare them guilty, O God! . . . Banish them for their many sins" (v. 10, NIV). The imprecatory psalms (curses on the wicked) sound anti-Christian to some believers. However, notice that David is not cursing *his* enemies, rather he is asking God to deal justly with those who have become enemies of *God*. These prayers stem from a deep love for God because of his mercy. Because of this, the one who prays this way cannot bear to see God's name profaned, so he prays that God would act justly for his own sake.

What moves you to pray against scandal in the workplace or lying by public officials or the persecution of Christians? Is it out of your own discomforts and fears that you might be next, or is it that you love God so much you cannot bear to see his holy name profaned?

Protective (vv. 11–12)

Finally, we are encouraged to come into God's presence because we can find protection in him. God "bless[es] the righteous," his own people (v. 12). God's blessings serve as a protective shield around the believer. It is because God's blessing surrounds his children that the righteous do not live in fear of the future. It is because of the surrounding of God's blessing that the righteous are not undone by the death of a loved one. Of course, believers will experience great trials and hardships on our long pilgrimage to glory (2 Corinthians 11:24–28), but in his kindness, God mysteriously intermixes our trials with his presence and blessings: "Many are the afflictions of the righteous, but the LORD delivers him out of them all" (Psalm 34:19; cf. 2 Corinthians 4:7–11). These are the truths we can live by: God's protection and provision of grace is certain.

The command to live by the truth does not imply that God is unconcerned about our feelings, however (v. 11). David prays that his people would "sing for joy"—that is, to feel the joy of God's care. Dare we ask God to confirm the reality of his promises to us in such a subjective fashion? This is precisely the kind of experience of grace he offers us, as Paul writes in Romans 8:16, "The Spirit bears witness with our spirit that we are children of God." God not only tells us we are his adopted children; through his Spirit he convinces us in such a way that we feel it—a reality that brings joy.

When my son Taylor was about five years old, my parents took him trick-or-treating in our neighborhood. I forgot to warn them that at the first house, the owner always greeted children with a scary mask. When they saw him, the mask was scary enough that it even startled my parents! When our masked neighbor saw Taylor, he came forward to offer him some candy.

Thinking Taylor would be terrified, my dad picked him up and held him close. But Taylor said, "I'm not scared, Papa; I recognize Mr. Charley's hands. Remember, he drives the fire truck!"

Boldly come into God's presence with all your petitions, because you recognize his hands. They are the ones that attentively respond, show mercy, work justice, and protect.

Questions for Reflection/Discussion

1. Which of the attributes of Jesus was the best news to you as you read?

2. What do these attributes reveal to you about how much Jesus values you?

3. How does this reality enable you to go to God in prayer?

Prayer

Consider a specific need or worry in your life right now, lifting this concern up to God. Reread Psalm 5 and thank God for the following truths:

- The Lord hears your voice (v. 3).
- His love is steadfast and abundant (v. 7).
- In the middle of your situation, you can trust him to lead you and make your way straight (v. 8).
- He is your protection and shield (vv. 11–12).

3

Deliverance from Depression

Psalm 6

Turn, O LORD, deliver my life;
save me for the sake of your steadfast love
(Psalm 6:4)

WHAT IF, AFTER meditating on the eternal blessedness of
Jesus's way in Psalm 1, you still have no joy? What if, after emp-
tying your heavy heart to Father as we learned in Psalm 5, you
still have no peace? What if you can't experience the hope that is
"poured into our hearts through the Holy Spirit" (Romans 5:5)?
David prayed Psalm 6 out of just such a crisis of faith. This psalm
is for those whose hearts are weighed down by spiritual battles,
disappointments, or unbelief. This psalm shows us how to cling
to the outpoured Spirit of hope even in the dark night of despair.

Martyn Lloyd-Jones called such despairing experiences *spiri-*
tual depression. In this way, he distinguished it from physiological
depression.[1] Some depression may need to be treated physically,
but all depression needs to be treated spiritually. As one who suf-
fers from both, I can testify to the Spirit's abiding comfort. Even
though medication has been a great gift of God's common grace
to help me remain balanced in my emotions, I can still lose sight
of God's promises. Medication, exercise, sunshine, and family

time assist my body and mind in fighting bouts of anxiety. But they cannot make me hopeful. They cannot provide peace *before* circumstances change. They cannot give me spiritual eyes to see Jesus sitting on his throne, ruling and reigning until he puts all enemies under his feet. Only the Spirit working by and with a passage like Psalm 6 can do that. This psalm is God's gracious gift to those who are depressed, who may have lost sight of him. God has used his Word to deliver me dramatically from a deep pit of despair, and he continues to deliver me daily from anxiety and hopelessness.

Oswald Chambers used to say that depression, or ordinary sadness, is part of being human; without it, no one would know what it means to experience joyful exaltation.[2] I have ministered to some people who were never depressed before they became Christians. They either lived in a kind of denial that ignored their own struggles or they had never known true elation and therefore never knew its opposite.

If sadness is necessary to being human, then we would expect our Savior to have also experienced this emotion. And as we read through the Gospels, we see Jesus grieving at Lazarus's tomb, weeping over Jerusalem, and agonizing in the garden of Gethsemane. But we also have the Psalms as a record of Jesus's prayers. Theologians have consistently said the psalms are the prayers of Christ spoken through the psalmists.[3] Dietrich Bonhoeffer said, "These same words which David spoke, therefore, the future Messiah spoke through him. The prayers of David were prayed also by Christ. Or better, Christ himself prayed them through his forerunner David."[4]

From the way Jesus quotes the Psalms in the Gospels, Bonhoeffer and others concluded that Jesus speaks the words of the psalms as his very own. Think of some common references you know. One is in this psalm: "Then I will tell them plainly, 'I never knew you. Away from me you evildoers!'" (Matthew 7:23, NIV; from Psalm 6:8). Or this one, "My God, My God, why have you forsaken me?" (Matthew 27:46, NIV; from Psalm 22:1).[5] In John 15:25 Jesus quotes Psalm 69:4 as his own words: "They hated me without reason" (NIV). This idea that the psalms are a record of the emotional struggles of our Savior will change the way you read and pray them. It will enable you to see an empathetic Savior who tasted every contour of the human experience. If we read that our Savior experienced grief and sadness then we too should view it as normal, even necessary, to experience the deep sadness of human brokenness. This reality leads us to respond in two ways: first, to hold on; second, to accept healing.

Hold On (vv. 1–7)

Depression often has a starting point; people are not usually born depressed. David's depression may have been situational since he mentions "enemies," perhaps they said or did something which sent him into a downward spiral. This is a reasonable inference since David had many enemies throughout his life. Among them were a giant who mocked him (1 Samuel 17:43); a king who was jealous of him (1 Samuel 18:29); a son who revolted against his government (2 Samuel 15:10); a counselor who joined a coup against him (2 Samuel 15:31); a descendent of Saul who cursed him (2 Samuel 16:5-8); and a friend who betrayed him (Psalm 41:9). In those moments he had nothing to hold on to, only God.

On the other hand, one can suffer from depression for no apparent cause. David mentions his enemies briefly at the end of the psalm, but he is consumed with the way he *feels*, he is primarily battling internal enemies of anxiety, hopelessness, and sadness. While skillful counselors have helped me identify contributing factors to my own depression through the years, there is no clearly identifiable cause. It is a thorn in the flesh the Savior has entrusted to me.

I can point to a particular day when my battle with depression began—a battle which crippled me for more than three years and has continued in various forms, especially as anxiety, even today. I was a child, standing on the playground of my elementary school across the street from my house. I loved school, and especially recess, but that day everything changed. I can't explain why, but the field in front of me became like a chasm separating me from my house, my parents, everything I had counted on for security. I became overcome with anxiety, which led to depression. Nothing in my life situation had changed except my perspective. In a moment, I was transformed from a happy-go-lucky kid to a heap of shivering nerves. I was fearful of teachers, fellow students, and any challenge. I was constantly weary and sad; and at the time, I didn't know I could hold on to God.

The anatomy of my depression closely resembled the one given in this psalm by David. Whatever happened, David inferred from his circumstances that God was punishing him, saying, "LORD, do not rebuke me in your anger or discipline me in your wrath" (v. 1, NIV). There were other times in David's life when he was correct; God was disciplining him for his sin and he was miserable until he repented (see 1 Samuel 11–12; Psalm 51). However, here David does not mention sin, which is atypical of psalms that express repentance. In verse 7 (NIV) he laments, "My eyes grow weak with sorrow; they fail because of all my foes." Something beyond his control—namely, the assault of his enemies—seems to have made him think God was angry with him. This was my conclusion in my depression, and it took years for me to be convinced otherwise. Maybe you can identify with this. We should not be too quick to conclude that depression is a sign of God's displeasure.

One commentator sympathizes: "For most sufferers, it is in the long watches of the night, when silence and loneliness increase and the warmth of human companionship is absent, that. . .pain and grief [reach] their darkest point."[6] In my depression, I hated the anticipation of bedtime.

A depressed believer can even feel God has deserted them. David often speaks of God as having hidden his face (Psalm 27:9;

102:2). Here he cries out, "How long?" He pleads for the Lord to "turn . . . and deliver [him]" and feels that death is imminent if he doesn't (vv. 4–5, NIV). In the lowest points of my depression, I remember being terrified of total abandonment, even to hell.

In Hosea 7:14, the Lord chided his people because they "wail on their beds" and "do not cry to [him] from the heart." No matter how dim David's faith became, it remained strong enough to cry out to God on the grounds of his redemptive love embodied in Jesus Christ. He cried, "have mercy on me, LORD, for I am faint" (v. 2, NIV). David was no weakling. Remember that earlier in life he killed a lion and bear with his own hands and a giant with a slingshot (1 Samuel 17:34–37, 48–49). He was a successful person and king of a powerful nation. Depression is not the disease of weak, unsuccessful people; it can beset anyone. In my own battle, I really thought I was losing my mind because the feelings I was having were so unlike me. Furthermore, I thought I was failing God. I supposed (wrongly) that he only wanted to use people who were strong.

In such times, we must appeal to God's mercy, that quality of character by which he compassionately draws the troubled close to himself. It was such a relief to me to discover this quality in God through passages like Psalm 103:14: "he knows how we are formed; he remembers that we are dust." It may have surprised and embarrassed me that I was fragile, but it did not surprise God. It should be a great encouragement to know that God is not surprised by our weakness, and that yet our unworthiness does not hinder his love for us. It was this idea that led the apostle Paul to be able to boast even in his weaknesses, because he was convinced it was in his weakness that he experienced God's strength. God gave him his "thorn in the flesh" to prove even more convincingly that the Lord's grace is sufficient (2 Corinthians 12:1–10).

Next, David appealed to God's loving-kindness, the very core of God's being (v. 4; cf. 1 John 4:8, 16). If we could reduce all of Scripture to one word, it would be this: *chesed*, or "unfailing love." Remember, when Moses asked God to reveal his glory, or his essence, this is what God showed him: "The LORD, the LORD, a God merciful and gracious, slow to anger, and abounding in steadfast love and faithfulness, keeping *steadfast love* for thousands, forgiving iniquity and transgression and sin" (Exodus 34:6–7, emphasis added). David knew this passage well and would repeat it in several other psalms. It is repeated throughout the Bible nine more times (Numbers 14:18; Nehemiah 9:17; Psalm 86:5, 15; 103:8; 145:8; Joel 2:13; Jonah 4:2; Nahum 1:3). What David was saying is the same thing you can say in your depression: "O Lord, however weak I am, I appeal to your unfailing love, which is greater than my depression."

Comfort in Your Affliction (vv. 8–10)

David encourages us with a record of his release from depression. What we are called to do in these verses may sound simplistic, but it is critical to accept God's comfort. I do not want to give the impression that if you perform a few simple steps your depression will go away. It may be that you will struggle on and off with it for the rest of your life, as have great saints of history like Martin Luther, John Bunyan, Charles Spurgeon, and William Cowper. Healing may include deliverance from all struggles with depression, but that might not happen right away or until you are with Jesus face-to-face. While God has provided inestimable grace to persevere through my many bouts with depression he has, for reasons sufficient to himself, chosen not to heal me completely. While I no longer experience depression or anxiety with hopelessness, I still struggle emotionally. You might continue to struggle as well, but the Lord will meet you in it as he did David. And I can testify with David, he has always met me. I would not treasure the Lord's presence as I do, nor believe the gospel as deeply as I do, had he not left this thorn in me. I am now able to say I am glad for this thorn and were I given a choice to be rid of it I think I would be the poorer for accepting the offer.

If you struggle with depression, sadness, hopeless, and anxiety—and all of us do at some times and to some degree—do not let those struggles drive you from Christ. Let them become a catalyst to drive you closer to the Lord. Receive the comfort and presence of trusted friends as from him. Drag yourself to corporate worship where the Lord can remind you of the gospel through word and sacrament. Even when the "darkness is [your] closest friend" (Psalm 88:18, NIV), remember by faith he is the "God who saves" (Psalm 88:1, NIV). "Come near to God and he will come near to you" (James 4:8, NIV).

The first step to receiving comfort in your affliction is to believe he hears your prayers. Though it may not feel like God hears us, we see David appeal to God's "unfailing love" (v. 4, NIV). God will never fail to hear the prayers of his children. This act of believing may sound logical and easy for some people, but for others it is a call to a hard obedience.

I remember a moment near the end of my severe depression when I was faced with a question: "Do I really want to get better?" On the one hand, I said, "That's a stupid question; of course I do!" On the other hand, it was not an easy choice, because I had derived some benefits from depression. I know that might sound odd, but it was true. I was let out of unpleasant activities and I received attention and sympathy from people. When I thought about it, I wasn't sure I wanted to get better and give up these things.

But there was an even more insidious reason I wasn't sure I wanted to get better: my depression had become part of my identity. My anger against God for allowing me to suffer like this, my sense of myself as a victim—these things felt like they were at the core of who I was. Was I willing to give up my anger and my identity as a victim to simply be a needy child of God? Not everyone who is depressed struggles with these questions, but I did. Suffering can become a wall we put up in order to keep God and others away from us. It can be strangely gratifying to claim to be angry with God, that God has been unfair, or that God has refused to help. It can be gratifying because we deeply love to go our own way, not God's way. For me to believe that God heard my cries, and to allow him to deliver me, would mean that I had to admit I was wrong about him—to admit he really was who he claimed to be.

Accepting God's comfort provides opportunity to brag on his mercy. It is important that when you experience relief from depression you acknowledge it to others. The psalmist says elsewhere, "Let the redeemed of the LORD say so" (Psalm 107:2). Tell someone you have been delivered. Not only is it necessary to give God the glory, but it helps in your future battles to recall that you were truly delivered.

The hopelessness of my battle with depression lifted during a hospitalization. Depression had wrecked my health. One day I was begging God to deliver me as I had done every day since it began. And he did. The cloud was lifted. I knew I was better, so I told the people attending to me that I was ready to go home. They couldn't believe it, so they called the psychologist to evaluate me. He leaned against the wall and asked me to tell him how I felt. As I told him that the Lord had delivered me, he slid down the wall and sat on the floor in disbelief. He told me to come to his office a week later. When I did, I was still better. He said he had never seen anything like it. In my regular bouts with anxiety and depression it always helps to recall this incident as an Ebenezer, a rock of remembrance of the Lord's deliverance.

Your experience with depression may be very different from mine. You may be healed permanently and never suffer again. You may never have a dramatic experience with despair. This is the way the Lord chose to work in my life. Regardless of the differences, we will all have at least some experience of sadness because we are united to Christ. Because Jesus prays this psalm on our behalf, we may be assured that our sadness is a necessary part of following him rather than a failure of faith. And as the Father gave his Son a joy deeper than his sorrow, he will do the same for us. Because of Jesus's past experience of the Father's faithfulness and his future hope in his resurrection, he was filled with joy in God's presence while he was still suffering (Acts 2:25–28; cf. Psalm 16:8–11). Jesus shares our humanity so he can "help those who are being tempted" or tested (Hebrews 2:18, NIV), and this help includes singing praises with us in the midst of our worship.

Questions for Reflection/Discussion

1. Did any of the experiences of depression listed resonate with your own experience? If so, how?

2. In what ways does depression drive us into deeper relationship with God?

3. How does the fact that Jesus draws near to his people in their suffering, rather than condemning them for their lack of faith, give you hope?

Prayer

Psalm 6 is a prayer for those struggling with depression. Use it as a guide to express your struggle to God, and ask him to give you hope and joy as you remember his nearness.

- Verses 1–7: Describe to the Lord the ways you are troubled and need deliverance.
- Verses 8–10: Write down all of the actions God takes toward David in his trouble. Praise God for how he hears your cries and comes near to you in the middle of your suffering.

4

Justice for the Desperate

Psalm 7

My shield is with God, who saves the upright in heart.
(Psalm 7:10)

FALSE ACCUSATIONS HAVE the potential to cripple even the strongest people. Sometimes only a handful of attacks can undercut the support someone has felt from many more. Even if I am vigorously supported by my church officers, generously loved by my family, regularly affirmed by my friends, and visibly appreciated by 99 percent of my congregation, one vicious letter has the potential to cripple me emotionally for a time. That one person's attack can make me feel like my whole world is collapsing and hinder my ability to listen to the many more who love me. Can you identify? I think most of us have had such an experience. One attacker can send us into a tailspin fearful our whole life is going to crumble.

That is where David is in this psalm. While Psalm 6 gives hope to those who cry out to Jesus when they are weighed down by depression, Psalm 7 gives peace to those who cry out to Jesus when they are being falsely accused. But this psalm gives us hope no matter what threat we are facing—whether from people or hard circumstances.

The superscription of Psalm 7 indicates that David wrote the psalm after an encounter with someone named Cush of the tribe of Benjamin; Saul, David's nemesis, was from the same tribe. Perhaps Cush was just another supporter of Saul who was falsely accusing David, but there is something about this accusation that is terrifying to David.[1] His prayer is desperate. Maybe he knew that if Cush's accusation got traction, it could unseat him as king, humiliate his family, or provoke foreign nations to war against him. Cush's accusation of David is the kind that will make a victim break out in a cold sweat, cause his eyes to flutter, his mind to whirl, and his body to twitch in the middle of the night. The only thing for weak people to do is to take hold of the same strong God David held on to.

Taking hold of God in prayer means that we can frankly express our fears like David, who is terrified of his enemies ripping him to pieces as fiercely as a "lion" (vv. 1–2). So far in the Psalter, this is David's most intense prayer. In Psalm 3, David is in physical danger, but for half of the psalm he displays quiet calm. In Psalm 4, he is distressed and only comes to peace by the end of the psalm. In Psalm 5, David is deeply wounded by the slander of his foes. By Psalm 6, David is deeply troubled and depressed. But this psalm's representation of his encounter with enemies is the lowest point we have experienced with David thus far.

However, David does not wait to gather himself before he talks to God. Like the psalmist, you and I can speak honestly with God right where we are.

What care do you need to cast honestly on him? Maybe it is a false accusation like that against David. It may be a disease or chronic pain. It could be a threat against your financial well-being. It could be someone's indiscretion that threatens your reputation. Whatever it is, pour it out to God with all its gory details. Then he can sustain you.

Charles Spurgeon lived and ministered in England in the nineteenth century. Though he was an extraordinarily gifted preacher who often exuded strength and confidence from the pulpit, Spurgeon knew how to pray honestly in private like David in the midst of pain and suffering. For most of his adult life he battled the agonizing pain of gout. In his autobiography, he records a heart-to-heart with God in the middle of a debilitating experience with the infection:

> I have found it a blessed thing, in my own experience, to plead before God that I am His child. When, some months ago, I was racked with pain to an extreme degree, so that I could no longer bear it without crying out, I asked all to go from the room, and leave me alone; and then I had nothing I could say to God but this, "Thou art my Father, and I am Thy child; and Thou, as a Father, art tender and full of mercy. I could not bear to see my child suffer as Thou makest me suffer; and if I saw him tormented as I am now, I would do what I could to help him and put my arms under him to sustain him. Wilt Thou hide Thy face from me, my Father? Wilt Thou still lay on me Thy heavy hand, and not give me a smile from Thy countenance?" . . . I bless God that ease came, and the racking pain never returned. Faith mastered it by laying hold upon God in His own revealed character— that character in which, in our darkest hour, we are best able to appreciate Him.[2]

The Father invites us to lay out our whole condition before him, to express the fullness of our anxiety and the entire desperation of our situation, because he stands ready to relieve us. David tells us in Psalm 55:22 (NIV): "Cast your cares on the LORD and he will sustain you." Notice that he does not say that he will sustain our *cares*; he will sustain *us*. When we pour out everything to our Father in prayer, we can experience this love.

To speak honestly with God is also to invite him to scrutinize our motives, as David pleads with God, "O LORD my God, if I have done this, if there is wrong in my hands . . . let the enemy pursue my soul and overtake it. . . . [J]udge me, O LORD, according to my righteousness" (vv. 3, 5, 8). David was evidently accused of taking advantage of someone who had been at peace with him earlier (cf. 1 Samuel 24:9). Instead of defending himself, David invites God to search out the matter. If he is guilty of the crime, he prays that God would allow him to be judged. The Roman Catholic biblical scholar Mitchell Dahood captures the intensity of David's prayer with his translation: "Let him trample my vitals in *Sheol*, let him cause my liver to dwell in the mud."[3] Such a prayer will certainly test the motives of your heart and the rightness of your actions!

This is David's way of asserting his innocence. He goes so far as to say that he is not only innocent of the outward crime, he is also innocent of any related motive, asking God, the one who "test[s] the minds and hearts" of people, to "[v]indicate" him according to his "integrity" (vv. 8–9, NIV). Some may think this is the epitome of arrogance. But there are other times when David is not so sure of his motives and invites God's scrutiny (Psalm 139:23–24). One can be outwardly innocent of a particular wrong of which one has been accused while still guilty of evil motives. Suppose someone at work accused you of saying something to his superior that kept him from getting a promotion. You know you are innocent of that charge. What do you do? Before you hire a lawyer, you take the matter to God and lay it out to him in detail. What would God find in your heart? Would he see that while you didn't lie about your colleague, you secretly hoped that he would get fired because you wanted his job? It is possible to be innocent in man's court and guilty in God's. If you want to grow and become increasingly free in your relationship with God, then invite him to scrutinize your heart.

In the second half of the psalm, David also prays for justice on the earth (vv. 6–7, 10–16). Personal trials can serve as an occasion to plead for God's wider purposes to be accomplished. C. S. Lewis said that when the Christian thinks of justice, he shudders because he only thinks of the judgment seat of Christ. But Lewis says we must not lose the Old Testament saints' perspective. The Old Testament believer viewed himself as a plaintiff rather than a defendant before God's throne, begging God to do right in the earth, not just forgive his sins. Old Testament judges were champions of right and liberators from oppression. They had this idea from God himself, who said in Isaiah 1:17 (NIV1984), "Seek justice, encourage the oppressed. Defend the cause of the fatherless, plead the case of the widow." The Messiah, when he came, would "judge the needy; with justice he will give decisions for the poor of the earth" (Isaiah 11:4, NIV). Therefore, when we are being unjustly attacked, we must ask the Lord to cause justice to prevail in the earth for his glory.

But before we go further, step back and observe something with me. How is David moved to pray beyond his personal situation? It is because he has God clearly before his eyes. David is utilizing his imagination, as Alexander Whyte would say.[4] He takes the time to place God in his mind's eye as he prays. He sees God seated on his throne, his bow "bent and readied" and his "deadly weapons" prepared for the "wicked man" (vv. 12–16). Rather than speaking idly to God, David shows us that we can get God before our eyes first. It will adjust our whole perspective, embolden our prayers, and make them more eternally significant.

It is common in David's suppliant psalms (psalms where he is asking God for something) to reach resolution by the end as he does here. David says, "I will give to the LORD the thanks due to his righteousness, and I will sing praise to the name of the LORD, the Most High" (v. 17). As far as we know, David said this before he saw earthly justice that vindicated his name. David received something greater—a fresh perspective of God.

Though David anticipated it, you have *seen* the ultimate display of God's righteous character: he forgave sins by justly punishing them in his Son. If God would endure the ultimate sacrifice, the loss of a son, in order to maintain justice, you can be assured he will one day right every other wrong.

My friend and mentor, Dr. Richard Chewning, was one of the very distinguished fathers of my denomination as well as an economist and professor of business ethics at Baylor University. After a Ponzi scheme had taken advantage of several of the Christian organizations he and I loved, I asked him how I should think about it all. This godly man said very calmly and confidently, "I will not allow it to make me a cynic or to quit trusting." He could say that because he had clearly, before his eyes, a God who had demonstrated his absolute justice through the cross. Jesus proved on the cross that God *will* execute justice, even if it means crucifying his own Son to do so. When we have this self-sacrificing God before our eyes, we can boldly go to him in prayer, asking him to work justice. Not all of our injustices will be righted in this life. However, we wait for an ultimate and ultimately *good* justice still to come.

Questions for Reflection/Discussion

1. Have you ever been falsely accused? What was the experience like?

2. Do you have hesitations about speaking to God honestly? If so, why?

3. What hope do we have that enables us to pour out our hearts to God in prayer in times of distress?

Prayer

Consider where you're being falsely accused or treated unfairly right now. Praying through the first seven verses of this Psalm can help bring peace to you even in the midst of those experiences.

- Verses 1–2: Describe the situation to God in detail. Though he already knows everything about your situation, Scripture encourages you to pour out your heart before him (see Psalm 62:8).

- Verses 3–5: Ask God to search your heart and reveal any ways you may be in sin with regard to this situation.
- Verses 6–7: Because he is angered at injustice, ask the Lord to deliver you from this situation.
- Verse 10: Praise God that he is your shield and you can trust in him to lead you.

5

The God You Can Know

Psalm 17

As for me, I shall behold your face in righteousness.
(Psalm 17:15)

HOW WELL DO you know God? Maybe a better question to ask ourselves is do we desire to know God? True success in this life will not be measured by accomplishment or acquisition. True success is reaching what you were created to do, and the ultimate thing we were created to do is to know God. As Jeremiah 9:23–24 (NIV) says, "Let not the wise boast of their wisdom or the strong boast of their strength or the rich boast of their riches, but let the one who boasts boast about this: that they have the understanding to know me." To know the Lord is to share in his life, to be joined with him through the loving reconciliation of God in Christ, through whom we also take on his characteristics so that we might imitate and glorify him. Every area of our lives is meant to lead us to a deeper knowledge of God. Relationships give more insight into his love. Careers and callings help us to understand more of his ways in the world. Life is about knowing God.

In Psalm 5, we saw that who Jesus is—a caring, attentive Savior—encourages us to go to him in prayer. In Psalm 7, we observed that when we get God clearly before our eyes, we are able to have peace, because he is a God who executes justice. Both of these important realities demonstrate that it is imperative that we know God. Psalm 17 shows us that God makes himself known to us and that knowing him is the source of true joy.

George Müller of Bristol, England built massive orphanages in the 1800s by trusting in God. Müller never developed a systematic means of raising money. He simply prayed, and God provided money, groceries, and workers. When he was in his eighties, someone asked him before a gathering of people what the secret to his success was. He struggled to his feet and lifted a pointed finger over his head and simply said, "I know my God, and my God knows me." Is your life one that will provoke someone to ask that question some day? Is it your passion now to know God? In Psalm 17, God entreats us to know him this intimately.

While each of the previous psalms is clearly a "prayer," this is the first one officially introduced as "A prayer of David." The editor who probably wrote this superscription wants to make sure that the readers know this is an inspired script to pray when one is in the fires of persecution. Surrounded by enemies who want to kill him, David the warrior's first response is to pray. Notice the intimate knowledge David has of God. It was through prayer that David had come to know God. Charles Spurgeon said as much: "David would not have been a man after God's own heart, if he had not been a man of prayer."[1] Praying this psalm will lead any believer to know God better.

Knowledge of God's Justice and Mercy (vv. 1–5)

In the first five verses, David shows us that to know God is to encounter him as a righteous judge. Knowing that God does not listen to the prayers of unrighteous people, David pleads his case: "Hear me, LORD, my plea is just; listen to my cry" (vv. 1–2, NIV). Appealing to a merciful God, he is convinced that God is righteous and will judge the case perfectly. You may not get a fair hearing anywhere else on earth, but you will with God. However, God is not like Lady Justice with eyes shielded from the person, only weighing the issue in her balance. He is the God of merciful justice who heeds the cry of the desperate.

As a righteous and merciful judge, God doesn't simply sit behind a desk; he *leads* his people in righteousness. God is glorified most by our bragging on the righteousness he has accomplished in us. Alexander Maclaren said, "[We] would be all the better for listening to the psalmist and aiming a little more vigorously and hopefully at being able to say, 'I know nothing against myself.'"[2] This God is a judge with whom you can have a personal relationship. Take your cause to him, whatever it is. If you do, you will discover him to be a merciful judge who is eager to deal with your case.

Knowledge of God's Love and Protection (vv. 6–9)

The proof that David knew God to be more than a judge enables him to move to the next section with ease. David calls on God as the great lover of his soul. Are you this confident of God's love for you that you would appeal to him to display it to the world? When we know God loves us, we are confident that he is eager to answer our prayers. When we know God loves us, we pray not merely to be delivered from trouble but in such a way that the wonder of his love is displayed to others. In fact, David is so confident in God's responsiveness to his children that he calls him the "Savior of those who seek refuge" (v. 7). David captures that provision of refuge to those who call on the Lord with two beautiful images.

The first image is a bit unfamiliar. David prays that God would keep him as the "apple of [his] eye" (v. 8). The apple of the eye is the pupil, the central point through which light enters our eye. There is no part of our body that we protect as carefully as our eyes; the very design of our eye sockets teaches us to do so. Listen to Spurgeon's artful description of that region of our anatomy:

The all-wise Creator has placed the eye in a well-protected position; it stands surrounded by projecting bones like Jerusalem encircled by mountains. Moreover, its great Author has surrounded it with many tunics of inward covering, besides the hedge of the eyebrows, the curtain of the eyelids, and the fence of the eyelashes; and, in addition to this, he has given to every man so high a value for his eyes, and so quick an apprehension of danger, that no member of the body is more faithfully cared for than the organ of sight.[3]

In a frightening way, our family once experienced how precious the eye is. I was pushing our twins in the stroller at the mall, when I heard them fussing. I walked around to the front of the stroller to discover that one of my daughters had removed a toy from the rack and had jammed it into her sister's eye. The victim was desperately trying to remove it while her sister was "helping." Somehow, I got the thing out, and then the blood began to flow. When we got to the emergency room and the attendants saw blood in the eye, they flung the doors open and put us in a trauma room immediately. In the end, there was no damage to the "apple of the eye," and with minor surgery she was fine. However, we were terror-stricken for hours, fearing that she would lose her sight, if not the whole eye.

When God loves you so much that he cherishes you as if you were the very pupil of his own eye, this same vigilant care is what he has in view. This God is one who loves you and who desires to be known. Take all your problems to him, and you will find one who is eager to reveal to you his cherishing love.

The second image we are familiar with: "hide me in the shadow of your wings" (v. 8). This is the image of a mother bird sheltering her young beneath her wings. We will see it again in Psalm 91:4 (NIV): "He will cover you with his feathers, and under his wings you will find refuge." He will even say that the child of God can "sing in the shadow of [God's] wings (Psalm 63:7, NIV).

On one occasion, when I was young, I spent a few weeks at my grandmother's house. During that time, I observed the happenings in a robin's nest next to my bedroom window. I watched the eggs hatch and the mother carefully gather food and bring it back to the constantly demanding babies. One day I saw a storm brewing on the horizon, so I went to the window to watch what would happen. The mother was there, sitting on her chirping babies. The closer the storm got the more she hunkered down on her babies. Finally, the storm hit her, the wind swept through her feathers and the large raindrops pelted her. The only movement she made was to blink the water out of her eyes. When the storm was over, she looked like she had been scraped on a washboard, but her babies were dry and secure. No storm can reach you without going through God first.

Knowledge of True Delight (vv. 10–15)

David's problems in this psalm are personal; he is encircled by heartless men. Look at the characteristics of David's enemies, and see if your enemies share the same. (If you're having difficulty doing this, expand your scope to include the troubles you're currently facing—cancer, family or work problems, or any other "enemies" you currently face.)

David's enemies have no pity. The text literally says that their hearts are "enclosed by fat." You may be at the mercy of some person or some agency which has no pity for you. They also "speak with arrogance" (v. 10). An enemy knows you are at his mercy, so he taunts you arrogantly. Like predators, they take advantage of David like a helpless animal: "They have tracked me down, they now surround me, with eyes alert, to throw me to the ground. They are like a lion hungry for prey, like a fierce lion crouching in cover" (vv. 11–12). This kind of enemy only wants your destruction. But while David is encircled by a solid wall of predators baring their fangs, he lifts his eyes above them and sees his beloved Father. He calls on God as a warrior, to brandish his sword and destroy his enemies.

The peculiar kind of warfare that the Lord will wage for us is intriguing. Verse 14 is difficult to translate. It seems best to translate the last part of the verse with the wicked as the subject of the sentence, continuing the idea that their "reward is in this life." So it would read, as the New American Standard Bible translates, "From men of the world, whose portion is in this life, and whose belly You fill with Your treasure; they are satisfied with children, and leave their abundance to their babes." It seems that David's enemies want something material that he has, so he prays that God would give them their fill of it. In effect he is saying, "They want this world; give it to them and let them perish in it. And further, if their children refuse to depart from their ways, fill them with it, too. Curse them with blessings." If they wanted money, David asks God to give it to them—along with all the emptiness that money alone brings. If they want his position, give them positions and all of the disappointment that position alone brings. C. S. Lewis said about such judgment:

> There are only two kinds of people in the end: those who say to God, "Thy will be done," and those to whom God says, in the end, "Thy will be done." All that are in Hell, choose it. Without that self-choice there could be no Hell. No soul that seriously and constantly desires joy will ever miss it. Those who seek, find. Those who knock, it is opened.[4]

A personal knowledge of God lifts your eyes above your enemies. And when that happens, you will hold less tightly to those earthly things that are being threatened. Let go of the fear that you will lose something material or time-bound. Let go of the race to be more prestigious than other people. Let go of your anger over those who threaten your property value. Let God give it to them, and in abundance, because that is their only reward. As we will see in the next verse, your reward will be fully received in heaven. The true reward for the person who has spent his life striving to know God will be in knowing him face-to-face (vv. 14–15).

Seeing God's face will be the final realization of what we were created to be. "As for me, I shall behold your face in righteousness; when I awake, I shall be satisfied with your likeness" (v. 15). Righteousness is more than a judicial state. In this case, it is conformity to the image or "likeness" of God. It is what John describes when he says that we "shall be like [Jesus] because we shall see him as he is" (1 John 3:2). The reward of seeing Christ, especially with resurrected bodies ("when I awake"), will involve a full transformation of our mortal, sinful selves into immortal perfection. We shall truly be sons and daughters of God because we will be perfectly conformed to the image of his Son. When you do see Christ and are conformed to his likeness, then the promise is that you will be satisfied. David is essentially repeating the same thing he said in his previous psalm: "you will fill me with joy in your presence, with eternal pleasures at your right hand" (Psalm 16:11). Knowing God and joy in the Christian life are intricately connected.

Henry Ward Beecher imagined that the Christian is being painted as a portrait, like Michelangelo's fresco on the ceiling of the Sistine Chapel. The Christian, like the chapel's ceiling during the days in which it was being painted, is encased in scaffolding. However, in that day when you shall see him, the scaffolding will be removed, and you will be satisfied with what he has done.[5]

So it will be in heaven for the Christian who has pursued knowing God. As great and longed for as they are, golden streets, mansions, old friends, and deceased relatives will not be the rewards. The face of the Lord Jesus Christ will be the only reward that satisfies for eternity. As Anne Cousin wrote,

The bride eyes not her garment, but her dear Bride-
    groom's face;
I will not gaze at glory, but on my King of grace;
Not at the crown he gifteth, but on his pierced hand:
The Lamb is all the glory of Emmanuel's land.[6]

Strive to know God, then, and rest assured that your hope will not be disappointed, not into all eternity. You will be filled with joy in his presence and eternal pleasures at his right hand.

Questions for Reflection/Discussion

    1. How is God simultaneously merciful and just?

    2. What images does this psalm provide that prove God's love and protection for his people?

    3. What is the only source of true joy, according to this psalm? What steps can you take to know God better?

Prayer

This psalm is about knowing God, a knowledge that gives us joy. Consider God's steadfast love (v. 7), the shadow of his wings (v. 8), and the hope and promise of one day seeing him face-to-face (v.15). How do these realities and the intimate knowledge of God help you experience joy in the midst of your circumstances? Spend some time prayerfully meditating over these truths.

6

The Victorious Death

Psalm 22

For he has not despised or scorned the suffering
of the afflicted one; he has not hidden his face from him
but has listened to his cry for help
(Psalm 22:24, NIV)

"ARE YOU AFRAID to die?" That was Barbara Walters' startling question to John Wayne in her much-anticipated interview of the "Duke." My dad and I, both huge John Wayne fans, had waited with eagerness for weeks to watch this conversation. But when Walters asked if Wayne feared death, my dad let out an expletive, sprang from his chair, and left the room. All I could hear as he made his way outside was, "It's none of her business! She has no business asking the man that kind of question!" For years afterward, whenever Barbara Walters appeared on television, my dad would complain about that interview and "that question."

It wasn't until I became a Christian as a middle schooler that I figured out why my dad had such a visceral response. He was terrified of death—his own as well as of those he loved. By reading some correspondence with one of his friends, I also discovered he battled deep anxieties over future suffering that could come on his family.

Dad became a Christian when I was in college. With a new heart for the Lord, he started reading and studying his Bible, a practice he continues today even with dementia. Recently I was sorting through some of his things in anticipation of his move to an assisted living facility. I was paging through some of his old, well-worn Bibles and cherishing the promises and principles throughout Scripture he had underlined or circled. It finally dawned on me he had not expressed a fear of death for years. And through many tragic twists and turns of his life in the last two decades, his peace and joy have been stunning to all of us. The realization was arresting. I have had the privilege of watching from a front-row seat what Jesus can do with a fearful, anxious person while he walks through the hardest things of life. Jesus clearly has spoken to my father in his later years, and my father has listened.

In chapter 1, we noted that Jesus is the truly blessed man who leads us through the Psalms. In Psalm 22, we see a Savior who leads us through suffering and gives us the victory over it. By being united to Jesus, his victory becomes our victory as well. Therefore, when we experience suffering, we are not commanded to become stronger to get through it; we are to cling to our suffering Savior, who leads us through it and gives us the victory.

So why would I be mentioning Christ so quickly when his name is not mentioned in this psalm? As you will see, this psalm has two sections which specifically prophesy what Christ would accomplish on the cross. The first half describes with poignancy his suffering, and the second half exuberantly proclaims his victory.

Suffering (vv. 1-20)

Jesus was nailed to the cross about nine o'clock in the morning and hung there until he was removed at three. From nine until noon he was tortured by people. Regardless of the mockery, scorn, and humiliation, Jesus did not retaliate. Instead, he ministered to others: he prayed, he asked John to take care of his mother, and he granted salvation to the thief beside him who begged for mercy.

However, at noon it all changed. Darkness covered the earth; the sun was eclipsed, cosmically reflecting what was happening to Jesus's soul. What he had suffered so far at the hands of human beings could not accomplish our salvation. He had to suffer under the hand of God. Isaiah 53:10 (NIV) says that it was not his body but his soul, "his life [was made] an offering for sin." Paul goes a step further and says that he was "made . . . to be sin" for us (2 Corinthians 5:21). It is this suffering that the psalmist explores in Psalm 22.

Forsaken (vv. 1–2)

One of the most obvious ways this psalm points to Jesus are the words of the first verse, the same words Jesus cried out on the cross: "My God, my God, why have you forsaken me?" God the Father poured out all the sins of his people on Jesus and then turned his back on him, because he cannot abide sin. How could it be that one person of the Trinity could forsake another and yet remain one God? It is difficult to understand. Luther said, "God forsaken by God, who can understand it?"[1] Occasionally I am asked if we really believed that Christ descended into hell as we confess in the Apostles' Creed. I say that we do not believe that he physically went to hell. However, he did experience all the torment of hell, which is being forsaken by God. It is right for someone to be disturbed by that thought; there is no way to mitigate the fact that he was forsaken by God because of our sin.

The Lord Jesus came to experience the entire human condition, even the experience of feeling forsaken by God. Jonathan Kozol relates a poignant expression by a woman who felt forsaken by God:

I don't pray! Pray for what? I been prayin' all my life and I'm still here. When I came to this [shelter] I still believed in God. I said: "Maybe God can help us to survive." I lost my faith. My hopes. And everything. Ain't nobody—no

God, no Jesus—gonna help us in no way. I do believe.
God forgive me. I believe he's there. But when he sees us
like this, I am wonderin' where is he? I am askin', Where
the [profanity deleted] he gone?"[2]

Perhaps you sometimes ask similar questions. When we feel
this way, we need to know two things. First, we need to realize the
presence of God through the personal ministry of God's people.
God may feel remote, but he is near to us through other Christians he uses to assure us. Secondly, we need to know that Christ
is still able to sympathize with those who feel abandoned by God.
He is the eternal proof that God goes to great lengths to draw near
to us in order to save us. Because God was "forsaken by God," we
can be assured that we never will be. His punishment, his death,
has bought peace with God for all who believe. The central promise of the Bible, "God is with you" is guaranteed by Jesus's life,
death, and resurrection.

Reduced (vv. 3–5, 9–10, 19–20)

Furthermore, Jesus was reduced to the point of begging God
to deliver him from his terror. He desperately pleaded with God
to deliver him just like he delivered his covenant people in the
past, saying, "In you our ancestors put their trust; they trusted
and you delivered them. To you they cried out and were saved"
(vv. 4–5, NIV). He pleads with God to care for him as he has
since birth: "From birth I was cast on you" (v. 10, NIV). And in
verses 19–20 he pleads for God to come quickly because he feels
as if he is being ripped apart by ravenous dogs. There is no other
way to say it: he is reduced to being a beggar.

It is incredibly traumatizing for a child to see a parent humbled by the terror of a marauder. Children who grew up in the
Holocaust describe with poignancy the specter of seeing a parent
forced to his or her knees desperately, humiliatingly begging for

their life. In Psalm 22 we see our Savior reduced to a beggar by the terror of evil, all because of our sin.

Tormented (vv. 6–8, 12–18)

While Jesus's greatest suffering was at the hand of God, his physical and emotional torment at the hands of men cannot be discounted.

Bleeds (v. 6). He bleeds and no one gives aid. No one extends pity to a worm oozing its life substance. So it is with Christ: a human being is bleeding from gaping wounds, and fellow humans merely stand and watch as if he were a worm. The word here is *tola*. The *tola* of Palestine and Syria was like the cochineal of Mexico, a little worm that feeds on cactus. Both in Mexico and Palestine these little worms are harvested and then crushed to extract their blood, from which the brilliant red garments characteristic of those two regions are made. Here the Savior is described as a worm crushed whose blood will clothe us in glory.[3] Sometimes anxiety sits so heavily on our chests that we feel our lives are being squeezed out of us. Jesus can still remember that feeling. Express it to him.

Mocked (vv. 7–8, 12–13). He is mocked by those who should be his friends. The very people he has wept over, the very ones he begged to come to him, now mock him: "He trusts in God. Let God rescue him now if he wants him, for he said, 'I am the Son of God'" (Matthew 27:43, NIV).

It is not just the uninformed populace; it is the religious leadership itself. The "bulls of Bashan" (v. 12) were the finest clean beasts that could be brought for sacrifice (Deuteronomy 32:14; Isaiah 2:13). They symbolize the religious leaders who knew the text we are studying, who knew that Jesus fulfilled all the predictions (Amos 4:1). Of everyone, they should have been his friends. Instead, they resent his disruption of their religious empire and tear at his soul like "roaring lions that tear their prey"

(v. 13). Betrayal by friends you thought were loyal is one of the most bitter wounds someone can experience. Only someone else who has been stabbed in the back can commiserate with you. Jesus has been betrayed, so he understands when you share that pain with him.

Died (vv. 14–16). Jesus completely experienced death. His body was racked with the pain of dislocated joints; his heart began to fail as he slowly suffocated; and he was desperately thirsty. If you have ever been at the bedside of a lucid dying human being, you know that their greatest luxury is simply moisture for their lips. Finally, he experienced the indignity of one whose possessions are divided before he dies. He endured it all because of our sins.

Whether you are suffering chronic physical pain, a slow debilitating illness, or are inching toward death, Jesus understands. He still bears the scars of his torture and remembers the terrors of his approach to the cross. None of your pain or fear will surprise or disappoint him. He knows how to comfort those following in his footsteps.

During the Holocaust, Dachau was used among other things for holding Christian ministers. Many of these gentlemen were stripped, stretched over a whipping block, strapped down with leather harnesses, and beaten until they were unconscious. Then they were tossed into a vermin-infested cell. It was the punishment for refusing to salute, attempting to celebrate communion, or protesting some Nazi atrocity.

The strategy was to break their souls, to transform them into animals. Many times it worked. These men were forced to beat each other. They fought each other for food scraps or outhouse privileges. They gave up and became animals; they became like their torturers in order to survive.

Jesus did not. Though his soul was crushed by God and his body and spirit were brutalized by men, he did not give up or become like his human tormentors. He gained the victory over sin and death, and his victory is your victory as well.

What does such sacrifice demand from us? Praise! The end of the passage says that those who recognize that he did this for them will proclaim his righteousness. If you have never recognized the price of your sin and have desired to be released from it so that you can live forever in fellowship with Jesus, then today you must ask him to apply what he did to you. If you ask him to do that, you will shout his praise at the realization of new life.

Victory (vv. 21–31)

There is a dramatic change of disposition that occurs between verses 20 and 21. However, it is a bit obscured by the NIV translation. The verb translated "save" is literally, "you have heard me." If translated that way, the verse would then read, "Rescue me from the mouth of the lions, from the horns of the wild oxen. You have heard me!" The Savior declares that he has been heard; a note of victory has been sounded. What is the victory? It is indicated by the verses that follow—he has won the salvation of his elect.

Family (vv. 21–30)

Jesus now declares to his people that he has achieved their salvation. Notice how he is transformed in his perspective from being completely alone, even separated from God, to being surrounded with new family members, saying, "I will declare your name to my people; in the assembly I will praise you" (v. 22, NIV). This is a remarkable portion of Scripture because it describes in triumphant terms the expansion of the gospel, which will occur in three phases.

Jews (vv. 22–24). The first phase of the application of what Jesus accomplished on the cross would occur among the Jews. That was God's design: to work salvation among the people that were closest to his heart, his first chosen people of the Old Testament. It was the order that Jesus decreed before his ascension, commanding that the gospel be carried to Jerusalem and Judea before going farther to Samaria and the Gentiles. It was the order that Paul practiced, going to the synagogues first and then to the Gentiles; this pattern is repeated numerous times throughout the book of Acts. Paul in fact declared that he was "not ashamed of the gospel, for it is the power of God . . . to the Jew first and also to the Greek" (Romans 1:16–17).

Gentiles (vv. 25–29). From the little congregation of brothers in verse 22, Jesus turns to a great assembly. Herein is described the next phase of the gospel mission: taking the good news to the Gentiles who have never heard. Jesus anticipated this day when the gospel invitation would go out to the Gentiles, inviting them to come to the feast of his grace. He told the story of the king who told his servants to go out to the highways and byways and invite them to his banquet (Matthew 22:1–14; Luke 14:15–24). Those were the Gentiles. He told another story about a man who had a vineyard and paid the workers hired last the same as the ones who worked all day (Matthew 20:1–16). Those hired last were the Gentiles who received the same grace as the Jews. In another place, he promised that he had other sheep not of this present Jewish fold (John 10:16).

You and me (v. 30). Finally, he sees all of his elect throughout the world down to the present day and beyond. In short, he saw you and me. The Lord Jesus did not endure the cross because he saw an indiscriminate mass of humanity that he hoped might believe in him. He died for his family, for those who would believe in him. What wondrous love that he would die not for a nameless mass, but for you and me, by name, by face! Surely it was this realization that caused Charles Wesley to write: "Died he for me who caused his pain, for me who him to death pursued! Amazing love, how can it be that thou my God shouldst die for me!"[4]

Finished (v. 31)

David concludes this psalm this way: "They will proclaim his righteousness, declaring to a people yet unborn: *He has done it!*" (v. 31, emphasis added). The final words of the verse were also repeated by Jesus on the cross when he said, "It is finished" (John 19:30).

Most every religion besides Christianity, and even some under the guise of Christianity, declare that one must atone for his own sins in whole or in part. Some teach that one must atone for his sins in order to avoid a worse reincarnation in the next life. Others prescribe self-atonement so that one can gain more wives, even a planet in the life to come. Others insist that atonement is procured through keeping the sacraments or through a certain quota of good works. In other words, in their minds, the work of atonement is never done. For some it is not even finished after one dies. In stark contrast to these beliefs, Jesus declared from the cross, "It is finished." He accomplished salvation. He covered the sins of all who will ask him to do so. If you have asked him, your sins are covered. There is nothing else to be done.

What will it mean then for your life that Christ has won you to his family and finished the work of atonement? You should never be concerned that you are a nobody, that no one cares for you, that your life is insignificant. When Jesus died, he died having known you from the foundation of the world. He endured the cross because he knew you, even the worst about you.

Psalm 22 shows us a Savior who can empathize with us when we suffer; he has suffered in every way. It shows us a Savior who died specifically to save you and me. It shows us a Savior whose death finished all the work necessary to save us and unite us to him. Therefore, through this union with him, his victory over suffering and death is our victory as well. We are not promised a life free from any suffering, but we are promised a Savior who will sustain us through it. We have the proof of it in this psalm.

Questions for Reflection/Discussion

1. When you are in the midst of suffering, do you feel that God is far away?

2. Where does this psalm tell us Christ is when we suffer? What does this tell you about Christ's love for you?

3. What is the proper response to receiving deliverance?

4. How might your own suffering better equip you to share Christ with others?

Prayer

Look very closely at how this psalm points you straight to Jesus. As you read, thank Jesus for suffering to save you, as well as for being with you in your own suffering. Meditate on the promise that he has not hidden his face from you and that he hears you when you call to him (v. 24). Let the comfort you receive from him propel you to prayerfully consider who else in your life needs to hear this reassuring truth.

7

I Believe . . . The Lord Is My Shepherd

Psalm 23

Surely goodness and mercy shall follow me all the days of my life, and I will dwell in the house of the LORD forever.

(Psalm 23:6)

PSALM 23 SERVES as the "bridge"[1] from the agonizing victory of Psalm 22 to the joyful exultation of Psalm 24, giving us hope in despair. In between those two states our Shepherd leads us to peace. Surely Psalm 23 is the most beloved psalm of all. Pastors and theologians throughout history have praised it consistently. J. J. Stewart Perowne, a commentator of the previous century, said, "There is no psalm in which the absence of all doubt, misgiving, fear [and] anxiety is so remarkable."[2] And while it is perhaps the most loved psalm, H. A. Ironside said it is also the "least believed."[3] However, to believe the words of Psalm 23 is to have peace—peace with God, peace in life, and the anticipation of peace in the life to come.

Peace with God

To know the Lord as your shepherd is to be at peace with God (v. 1). The amazing combination of words in the first verse of this psalm begins to show us why we can have peace with God: "The

Lord is my shepherd." Lord is the translation of God's personal name, which literally means "I Am who I Am." It is the name by which God revealed himself to Moses in the burning bush (Exodus 3:14) and the name he used about four thousand times in the Old Testament. On the one hand, Lord communicates the eternal and immutable nature of God—he has no beginning and no end. On the other hand, it reveals the self-sufficiency of God (what theologians call "aseity"). He depends on no one for life or power or accomplishment. These three core characteristics—eternity, immutability, and aseity—express who our God is. The *Westminster Shorter Catechism* reflects this mystery when it defines God as "infinite, eternal and unchangeable in his being, wisdom, power, holiness, justice, goodness and truth" (Question 4).

Notice, however, that God is not only revealed as the Lord; he also calls himself a shepherd. A shepherd in an agrarian culture of David's day was at the bottom of the cultural ladder. Nobody aspired to be a shepherd. If a family needed a shepherd, the task was dumped on the youngest son, as it was with David (1 Samuel 16:11). The shepherd lived with the sheep in order to protect the senseless animals from harm, and his work was endless. It was hard, lowly work, but it was nevertheless a work of protection and care. And it is this work with which the Lord, the timeless and self-sufficient ruler of the universe, chose to identify himself as the one who cared for Israel (cf. Psalm 80:1). The greatest over all identifies as the lowest servant.

Living on this side of the New Testament, we understand our shepherding Lord in a deeper way. We do not merely have Psalm 23 to help us understand God's care for us; we have the personal image of Christ, who regularly calls himself our shepherd. In John 10:11, he says, "I am the good shepherd. The good shepherd lays down his life for the sheep." In Luke 15:3–7, Jesus defends his mingling with tax collectors and sinners by explaining that he is a shepherd that goes after his lost sheep (cf. Matthew 18:12–14).

In Hebrews 13:20, the Lord is "the great shepherd" who has risen from the dead to restore life to his sheep. In 1 Peter 5:4, Christ is called the "chief Shepherd" who will someday return and gather his fold to himself. He is the dying, rising, seeking, restoring, returning Shepherd.

Notice how all of those verbs have *us* in view; he does all of those things for us as his children. The Lord has become *our* saving shepherd! He is the one who can forgive your sins, reconcile you to God, and lead you into God's family. If you will embrace the great Shepherd by believing in him, this great servant will work peace between you and God.

Peace in Life

David says, "The LORD is my shepherd, I lack nothing" (v. 1, NIV). To believe the Lord is our Shepherd is also to know peace in life, the provision for our every need (vv. 2–5). All the images David provides in this psalm concerning the shepherd's provision are fulfilled in Jesus. Jesus tells us his "little flock" not to be afraid because he will supply our material needs (Luke 12:22–32). Through his Spirit, Jesus "leads . . . beside quiet waters," by "guid[ing us] into all the truth" (John 16:13). "Do not let your hearts be troubled" by death, the Good Shepherd says, because he goes through the valley of the shadow in order to "prepare a place" for us in heaven (John 14:1–3, NIV). Instead of provoking dread, his "rod and . . . staff" comfort us because we know our ruler shepherds his people (Matthew 2:6). And the abundant table of grace Jesus spreads for his people so fills them they can even love their enemies (Matthew 5:44). Therefore, if you are in Christ, you can be assured that every need you have will be met. He will provide for you.

Notice, however, that the resting "beside quiet waters" mentioned in verse 2 (NIV) is a rest that requires the shepherd's intervention. Sheep may not always lie down to rest on their own. In the 1970s Phillip Keller wrote what has become a classic on Psalm 23. Keller grew up in east Africa observing shepherds, and was himself a sheep rancher for eight years before becoming a pastor. He observed that sheep need four things before they will rest. They need to be free of the fear of enemies; they need to be free of the friction that comes from the more aggressive sheep establishing the "butting order"; they need to be free of flies; and they must have full stomachs. Fear, friction, flies, and famine.[4]

Our Good Shepherd invites us to rest, but not without addressing these obstacles to our rest. To our fear he says, "Do not be afraid, for I am with you" (Genesis 26:24, NIV). To our friction he says, "Live at peace with each other" (1 Thessalonians 5:13, NIV). To the "flies" that disturb our peace—the suffering and pain that are inescapable in this present life—he says, "this light momentary affliction is preparing for us an eternal weight of glory beyond all comparison" (2 Corinthians 4:17). Living out Psalm 23 means that we actively seek rest from the Lord—and reject trying to find rest on our own and by our own strength. It means consciously entering his presence to experience the peace he offers. It means calling out to your Good Shepherd for help. It means thanking him for the help he provides. It means reading and rereading this psalm (and others), feeding on God's Word by studying it to claim God's promises for you and yours. This is the way of peace.

F. W. Boreham related a story he heard from a chaplain named Gault who ministered to men on the battlefront in France during World War I. Before each soldier left for the front, Chaplain Gault would teach him a simple way to remember Psalm 23:1. He would have him tick off the words to the first line using his fingers. The pinkie represented the word *The;* the next finger, *Lord;* the next, *is;* the index finger, *my;* and the thumb, *shepherd.* He would then have each man write the verse on his palm with an indelible marker, especially emphasizing the index finger, which represented the Lord's personal care promised in the psalm. After the second battle of Bullecourt, one of Gault's disciples was found dead . . . grasping with his right hand the *index* finger of his left.[5]

Restoration. The one who believes Christ is his shepherd will experience the restoration Christ brings. Keller says that one of a sheep's greatest enemies is itself. Often because a sheep is too fat, or has too much wool, or has just found a soft low place in the ground, she will "cast." That is, she will roll over on her back and be unable to right herself. If not rescued, gases will build up in the rumen and cut off blood flow. On a hot day, a sheep can die in a few hours. The shepherd, therefore, must constantly count his sheep, making sure each one is upright.[6]

The Savior is in the habit of giving our lives back to us. He demonstrated this when he saved us, having pity on us because we were downcast, "like sheep without a shepherd" (Matthew 9:36). Like sheep, we often live as enemies to ourselves because of our inherent sinfulness. Like a devoted shepherd, Jesus constantly pursues and restores us, just as he restored Peter, saying, "Do you love me? . . . Feed my sheep" (John 21:17). When he meets us in our sin, he restores our love and sets us back on the path of service.

Guidance. When you believe that Christ is your Shepherd, you will never lack guidance (vv. 3–4). A good shepherd creates a predetermined grazing plan so that no pasture becomes over-grazed and so that the sheep constantly have sufficient food. Our Shepherd promises to lead us in righteousness, the right way, the way he has determined from the foundation of the world. It is not always straight or easy—it sometimes involves wandering or suffering—but it is always best. We are assured that he does not lead us carelessly either. It is "for his name's sake" (v. 3), and therefore his reputation is on the line. David emotionally describes the inexplicable peace the Lord provides for his children, often through the ordinary means of grace he places at our disposal. As we have seen already, through his Word, he reminds us of who he is because he knows we are prone to forget his character and his promises. Through prayer, he invites us to pour out our pains and claim his promises.

The psalmist does acknowledge the difficulty of the path. The Hebrew phrase in verse 4 is better rendered "darkest valley," which would certainly include death, but all of life's other difficulties too, which can sometimes seem worse than death. Keller says that a good shepherd, when leading his sheep through the mountains, always goes through the valleys for three reasons: it is the gentlest way of ascending to the heights, valleys are well watered, and the best forage is there.[7]

To go on to higher places in Christian maturity, Christ must lead us through difficulties. Though they are excruciating, they do not last forever. There is dancing after mourning (Psalm 30:11). There is also purpose in our difficulties. God uses our suffering to make us a comfort to others, but he must first cut ditches in our lives through which the water of his healing will flow. He must wound us to make us healers (2 Corinthians 1:3–7). In this way, even our difficulties are used for good. "You prepare a table before me in the presence of my enemies," David writes, "you anoint my head with oil; my cup overflows" (v. 5). In other words, Psalm 23 suggests that the Christian who lives in the knowledge of his Shepherd's care will know inexplicable sustenance in the midst of his suffering. The Lord's sheep will marvel at how unbelievers could possibly live without the hope the believer has that God will one day "wipe away every tear from their eyes" (Revelation 21:4).

Safety. The one who knows the Shepherd never lacks ultimate safety. Though we are not promised physical safety in this life, we are promised the presence of God in our lives and the eternal security of our souls. Ultimately, we will live with God forever in a renewed creation where there *will* be perfect safety in every way (Revelation 21:1–4).

Two tools are described in verse 4—the "rod" and the "staff" of the shepherd.[8] The rod was the essence of the shepherd's power and authority. A skillful shepherd could use his rod as a weapon and sling it with great accuracy. The staff is a symbol of comfort. A shepherd could use its crook to draw wandering sheep together for warmth; he could pull an entangled sheep from the brambles; or sometimes he would simply touch a frightened sheep to assure him of his presence.

The Word of God serves these functions in our lives as well. Its teachings enable us to fend off the would-be assailants of false worldviews. Its warnings rebuke us when we wander into disobedience. And its promises pull us together as a church family, deliver us from despair, and assure us of Christ's presence.

Provision. Another theme of Psalm 23 is that of provision. Keller theorizes that it is not accidental that common regions for sheep herding—like East Africa, the Western United States, and Southern Europe—refer to high plateaus as "mesas" or tables. He takes this as a description of the shepherd's preparation of a pasture for summer grazing. Keller and his son would carefully walk through the fields and pluck out the poisonous white camas, plants which could paralyze young lambs. He also describes his use of oil to protect his sheep's heads and nostrils from flies, to grease the horns of rams so that they didn't kill each other when ramming, and to treat scabs that could spread to the flock. Keller also kept a decanter of brandy that he would use on cold days to revive a faltering lamb whose coat was not thick enough to keep him warm.[9]

Likewise, our Savior has gone before us by means of his Word, giving us everything we need for a life of godliness (2 Peter 1:3). His living life in our place, experiencing every trial, and suffering the worst of death enables him to have a cup of comfort that overflows to us. There is nothing that we can experience that he has not already conquered in order that he might make provision for us in the midst of it.

Peace in the Life to Come

Finally, the one who knows Christ as his shepherd can face the life to come with peace: "I shall dwell in the house of the LORD forever," David says (v. 6). We have been exploring the manifold faces of Christ's goodness and love expressed in his leadership, but notice that goodness and love are blessings that will be passed on by those who are his sheep.

Those who follow Jesus, conscious of his goodness and love, will inevitably bless those who follow him with the same. When we see our lives with the Lord as sitting at a table heavily laden with mercies, that will take our minds off ourselves and inspire us to share Christ with others. However, if we are constantly complaining about how bad our lot is in life, looking only to the fulfillment of our own needs and complaining about our meager experience of grace, we will not bless others nor leave a legacy of generosity. C. S. Lewis said, "Aim at heaven and you get earth thrown in. Aim at earth and you get neither."[10] Aim at a heavenly perspective of God's mercy to you and you will have goodness and love to leave behind to those who remain on earth after you pass into the next life.

The call, then, is to focus on dwelling with Christ in his house. Heaven should be a part of our everyday thoughts: "How do I want what I do today to be viewed in heaven?" "How important is this purchase in view of heaven?" "I will not fear this medical report because heaven is my home." How different our lives would be if we more consciously lived in the presence of our Shepherd? Such thoughts can transform even the most unacclaimed lives into ones rich in goodness and love.

John Bunyan includes in his *Pilgrim's Progress* a description of a poor fellow named Mr. Feeble-Mind. Regardless of his weakness, he had plenty of grace to share with others because of his hope of heaven. He says at one point: "But this I have resolved on, to wit, to run when I can, to go when I cannot run, and to creep when I cannot go. . . . My mind is beyond the river that has no bridge, though I am, as you see, but of a feeble mind."[11] Do you want to be at peace in this world and lead others to that same peace with you? You don't have to be great. Just set your mind, regardless of how feeble, on your heavenly home and then live consciously in that knowledge.

Shortly after World War II, the Allied forces gathered many hungry, homeless children and placed them in large camps. Even though they were given warm beds, plenty of clothes, and ample food, the children were restless and slept only fitfully. A psychologist finally came up with an idea. After each child was put to bed, he or she was given a slice of bread to hold. If they wanted more to eat, it would be given, but this one was only to hold. The children fell fast asleep, assured that they had something to eat the next day.[12] Psalm 23 provides us assurance of God's loving, attendant care for us. We love this psalm, but do we believe it? Psalm 23 is intended by the Great Shepherd to assure you of his provision, not just for today and tomorrow, but "forever" (v. 6). Because you are assured of your Shepherd's everlasting provision, you can have peace.

Questions for Reflection/Discussion

1. David says in verse 1 (NIV), "I lack nothing." He proceeds to describe how Christ, our shepherd, meets all of our needs. Which description of Christ's provision most resonated with you? Why?

2. What proof has Christ given you that he will indeed provide for you in all these ways?

3. With this in mind, how should we respond when we feel a lack of peace?

Prayer

This is a great psalm to memorize. In fact, you may know it by heart already. Pray through each verse of this short psalm, thanking God for each of the ways he provides for you, and ask him to give you peace in the knowledge that Jesus is your Great Shepherd described here. If you're facing a valley right now, meditate further on this psalm, considering how each verse describes God's love, care, and provision for you during this time.

8

Four Prayers,
Four Promises

Psalm 25

To you, O LORD, I lift up my soul.
(Psalm 25:1)

ONE OF THE most important things about a person is where
she turns in the midst of chaos. You can probably think of a few
things right now that cause you stress or anxiety. God has given
us many resources in his common grace, but nothing that God
has given us must be the *first* place we turn. While it may sound
simplistic, the psalmist tells us we must first turn to God. We can
only survive the chaos we experience by fleeing to God constantly
in prayer based upon his promises. Psalm 23 shows us the Good
Shepherd to whom we must turn. In Psalm 25, David shows us
why he turned to this Good Shepherd in his dangerous world,
and he commends to us the same.

It is easy to get discouraged. In his commentary on this passage, Charles Spurgeon said that in discouraging times, faith is
the "lever by which we lift our heavy hearts up to God in prayer."
However, he went on to say, it is a load too heavy with all of our
tugging to move. We would be utterly defeated unless "the heavenly lodestone" of Christ's love with its omnipotent powers pulls

our hearts upward.[1] In other words, Christ's love is like a giant magnet that pulls our hearts out of the trash heap of doubt and up to God through prayer based on his promises.

In this psalm, David acknowledges four promises regarding God's trustworthiness, guidance, friendship, and redemption. These promises apply to you as well. Based on these promises, David makes four prayers, demonstrating that we can go to God in prayer based on his promises.

God Is Trustworthy (vv. 1–3)

David entrusts his soul to God and prays that God would not let him be ashamed. The biblical concept of shame is a bit different from our American idea. Our idea of shame is embarrassment. The Bible certainly addresses that emotion when Jesus warns that we must not be ashamed of his coming lest he be ashamed of us (Luke 9:26), and when Paul declares that he is not ashamed of the gospel in Romans 1:16. However, this is not the predominant idea of shame. In the Bible, shame usually refers to being disappointed, let down, or abandoned. For instance, in Isaiah 49:23, the King James Version reads, "they shall not be *ashamed* that wait for me" (emphasis added; cf. 28:16; Romans 9:33; 10:11). The NIV translates it: "those who hope in me will not be disappointed." In Romans 5:5, Paul says that the Christian has a "hope that maketh not *ashamed*" (KJV). Again, the NIV (1984) translates, "hope does not disappoint us." When David says, "O my God, in you I trust; let me not be put to shame" (v. 2), he is begging God not to leave or abandon him. The positive prayer would be, "Be near to me!"

Immediately after making this petition, David declares the promise that God is trustworthy: "Indeed, none who wait for you shall be put to shame" (v. 3). The fact that David prayed *before* he remembered God's trustworthiness is instructive. When we pray first, our faces and ears are toward the Lord, which positions us to see and hear his encouragement. The promise is this: the one who looks to God for salvation from all troubles will never be abandoned or disappointed. The opposite is also true: the one who looks anywhere else will *always* be disappointed. God insists that we call on him for help because our sin causes asking for help to be contrary to our nature. We either want to repair things ourselves or we want to wallow in our self-pity. So God says in effect, "Contrary to your sinful inclinations to not ask for help, turn to me. You will not only be comforted with a promise; you will not be disappointed."

God Will Guide You (vv. 4–10)

David makes this point artistically with an acrostic. In an acrostic psalm, each line begins with a successive letter of the Hebrew alphabet. Psalmists use acrostics for different purposes. It seems that David's purpose in this case is to remind the believer of the necessity of basic guidance and instruction from God throughout life. In other words, God is saying, "Let me teach you the ABCs of getting through life." David prays for God to "show" and "teach" his "paths" (v. 4, NIV), as well as to "guide" (v. 5, NIV). God is described as one who "instructs sinners in his ways" (v. 8, NIV) and who "teaches them his way" (v. 9, NIV).

Notice by using the plural "ways" and "paths," David is not coming to God for guidance in just one area of his life. He desires to have a comprehensively obedient life. Therefore, he asks God to guide him *all* of his days. Whereas we often only want the Lord to guide in one particular area (particularly if it benefits us), we must yield the whole of our lives to him for total obedience.

To yield our lives to God in total obedience requires humility. When we pray for guidance, God gives us his Word where we can seek it. God primarily guides his children through Scripture. There is no point in praying for his guidance for the rearing of your family, the conduct of your business, or the character of your life unless you are willing to humble yourself and read his Word to find it (Psalm 119:105).

As we humble ourselves before God's Word, we can expect that our sins will be exposed. Rather than becoming defeated by them and withdrawing from God in shame, let us confess our sins to God, knowing that he has forgiven us in Christ. David is penitent as he makes his pleas. He cries out to God saying, "Do not remember the sins of my youth" (v. 7, NIV); "forgive my iniquity" (v. 11, NIV); and "take away all my sins" (v. 18, NIV). We do not deserve God's guidance, and yet he provides it as a gift of grace. To be guided by him involves walking in a constant posture of repentance and, turning away from rebellion, selfishness, and pride and turning toward Jesus, the victor over sin and death, in faith. Remember, his victory is our victory!

Notice that David's attitude and his petitions are based on God's promises. God is "[g]ood and upright" (v. 8), which is to say, merciful and just. Because of this, he can instruct sinners in righteousness. How can God be just—giving sinners what they deserve—and still be merciful? On the other hand, how can God be merciful and not compromise his justice? The answer, of course, is found in Jesus Christ. When Jesus died, he took upon himself the just wrath of God against sin. With sin justly dealt with, there is no hint of wrong in God's extension of mercy to the repentant.

It can be a struggle to believe in this grace God gives us. In his commentary on this psalm, H. A. Ironside tells the story about a man he once ministered to. Though the man had been a Christian for most of his life, at the age of ninety he asked Ironside to help him. "Everything seems so dark," the man told him. Ironside reminded the man of the many years he had walked with Christ and what a blessing he has been to others. Still, the man could not accept God's grace: "Yes," he said, "but in my illness, since I have been lying here so weak my memory keeps bringing up the sins of my youth, and I cannot get them out of my mind. They keep crowding in upon me, and I cannot help thinking of them; they make me so miserable and wretched."[2]

Ironside turned to verse 7 of Psalm 25 (KJV): "Remember not the sins of my youth, nor my transgressions; according to thy mercy remember me for thy goodness' sake, O LORD." Having read the verse, he asked the man if he had, like the psalmist, confessed his sins to God. "I am afraid," the man said, "that I forgot some of them." Ironside replied:

> "It is not a question of being able to remember every individual sin. You acknowledged that your life had been a life of sin, and do you not remember what happened then?" His mind was very weak, and I said, "Don't you remember that when you confessed your sins, God said, 'Their sins and iniquities will I remember no more'? If God has forgotten them, why should you think about them?"
>
> He looked at me and smiled and said, "*I am an old fool remembering what God has forgotten.*" So he rested on the word of the Lord and was at peace.[3]

If we have faith in Christ, we must think of our sins as God does.

Next, David's attitude and petition are shaped by God's promise to lead and teach the humble (v. 9). It is simple: if you humble yourself to be guided, God will guide you. Remember, the Bible teaches that the reason we worry is that we are proud. We become overwhelmed when we feel out of control, which exposes that we think we can control our lives. Peter says, "Humble yourselves therefore under the mighty hand of God . . . casting all your anxieties upon him, because he cares for you" (1 Peter 5:6–7).

Finally, God's steadfast love and faithfulness cause David to desire to be comprehensively obedient: "All the ways of the LORD are loving and faithful toward those who keep the demands of his covenant" (v. 10, NIV). Sometimes we are reluctant to submit to God because we are afraid he will take us in a harmful direction. All of our Father's ways are loving and faithful. You can completely abandon yourself in obedience to one who has proven in Christ that he will never harm or shame you.

The next prayer begs God for forgiveness of a great sin. It is clear from David's life that one of the ways he recognized the depth of the Savior's love was by being forgiven of "great" "iniquity" (v. 11, NIV). If you don't recognize how many debts Jesus has forgiven, you will not appreciate the treasures of his love. Remember the story in Luke of the "sinful woman" who interrupted the dinner meeting Jesus was having with Simon the Pharisee? She abandoned all social protocol and washed Jesus's feet with her tears, then dried them with her hair. Simon was aghast, but Jesus explained that the reason she displayed such affection was because she had recognized how much forgiveness she had received—while Simon, who owed the same sin debt, showed Jesus little hospitality because he thought he needed nothing from a Savior (Luke 7:36–50). The one who recognizes she has been forgiven much loves much, while the one who thinks she needs to be forgiven little loves little.

Confession is a means of grace we tend to neglect. James presses us to confess our sins to one another, and at times confess our sins to our elders (James 5:13–20). Someone once made a request of Charles Wesley: "I want you to pray for me, I am a really great sinner." So Wesley prayed, "O Lord we pray for this poor sister. She is a great sinner." Indignantly she took him by the arm and said, "Stop! Who has been telling you about me?"[4] She didn't really believe she was a great sinner; it was merely a ploy to get people to tell her how great she was. We will never move on in the Christian life until we recognize that we really are great sinners. We will only discover the depth of Christ's love to the degree that we confess to him the depths of our depravity.

God Will Befriend You (vv. 12–15)

P. C. Craigie said, "The essence of the road of the righteous is this: it is a road too difficult to walk without the companionship and friendship of God."[5] Far from using your sin against you, God promises to come close when you confess. After his tragic sins of adultery and murder, David prayed not for re-salvation but restoration of the "joy of your salvation" (Psalm 51:12). The *Westminster Confession of Faith* captures this biblical teaching this way: "God continues to forgive the sins of those who are justified. Although they can never fall from the state of justification, they may by their sins come under God's fatherly displeasure and not have a sense of his presence with them until they humble themselves, confess their sins, ask for forgiveness, and renew their faith in repentance."[6] Elsewhere a psalmist also describes the restoration of fellowship with the Father upon repentance, "I will punish their sin with the rod, their iniquity with flogging; but I will not take my love from him, nor will I ever betray my faithfulness" (Psalm 89:32–33, NIV). That loving friendship is also based on respect. It is the one who "fear[s] the LORD" who is instructed in this way (v. 12, NIV), who experiences "prosperity"—an overall fruitful life and godly "descendants" (v. 13, NIV)—and whose "feet" are kept "from the snare" of sin (v. 15, NIV).

God Will Completely Redeem (vv. 16–22)

There is a fourth prayer in verses 16–22. However, if you look closely at it, you will see that it really is a reiteration of the three prayers we have just studied. Verses 16–18 comprise the prayer to forgive; verses 19–20a make up a prayer for God to guide out of trouble; and verses 20b–22 form a prayer for God to deliver from shame all of his elect through the ages. This one is the most urgent, like a frightened child in a swimming pool pleading, "Don't drop me, Daddy!"

I said at the beginning that there are four prayers in this psalm accompanied by four promises. While it may seem that the psalm lacks an immediate promise following verse 22, the promise that follows this final prayer for total redemption is the rest of the Bible, which promises that God will completely redeem the world. Jesus is the promise given in answer to this prayer, and salvation through him is preached from the beginning to the end of the Bible.

As a devotional, Martin Luther was reading to his family the story of God's calling Abraham to sacrifice his only covenant son, Isaac. In the middle of the story, Luther's wife Katie protested, "God would never do that; he would never kill a son!" Luther responded, "But Katie, he did."[7] He killed his own so that Abraham would not have to kill his.

At the beginning of the chapter, I asked you to reflect on the things that cause you stress or anxiety. Of what comfort is this promise in view of the tragic world we live in? It would be of no comfort if the God who made these promises had never experienced pain. But that is not the case. All of God's promises are "yes" and "amen" to us in Christ (2 Corinthians 1:20), the Son whom God offered up on our behalf. God has promised to forgive; he has promised to guide his people out of trouble; and he has promised to deliver all his children from shame. Because he makes these promises, we can turn to him in prayer.

Questions for Reflection/Discussion

1. *Trustworthiness*: What promise does this psalm give regarding God's trustworthiness? Why is it so important that we turn to God in times of distress?

2. *Guidance*: Why does accepting God's guidance require repentance on our part? How can you take hold of God's promise to guide you?

3. *Friendship*: How does God's friendship enable us to repent?

4. *Redemption*: Where else in the Bible do you see evidences of God's promise to redeem all things? How does God's promise to redeem embolden you to pray?

Prayer

Which of the four promises in this psalm do you need most right now, and why? (It doesn't have to be just one of them.) Spend time praying and asking God to meet your needs based on his trustworthiness, guidance, friendship, and redemption. Ask him to show you your next step to take in faith, in light of these promises.

9

When Accused

Psalm 26

My foot stands on level ground;
in the great assembly I will bless the LORD.
(Psalm 26:12)

GOD'S PROMISES NOT only embolden us to pray to him, but also give us peace when we are being accused. All four of the promises noted in Psalm 25 had God as the actor. That means no matter what accusations come our way, we can point to what God is doing in our lives as far more important and substantial than whatever we are being accused of. The most important promise to cling to when accused is the promise that God will give you the righteousness of Christ when you put your faith in him. It is the only promise secure enough to sustain us through accusations.

Accusations can come from many sources. Satan makes accusations against us to God (Revelation 12:9–10). Our own consciences constantly assail us with feelings of inadequacy, shame, and the desire for others' approval. And the accusations of other people have the propensity to be debilitating. To survive such accusations, we need a firm foundation on which to stand.

Archimedes (c. 287–212 BC) was a Greek mathematician and inventor. He was so certain of his conclusions from his study of levers that he once boasted, "Give me a place where I may stand,

and I will move the earth." His claim was that if he had a solid base outside the earth on which to place his fulcrum, then he could place one end of his lever under the earth, push on the other end, and move the earth from its orbit. Of course, Archimedes was speaking rhetorically. But his point was that a firm foundation is a source of power.

If your life is not built on the solid foundation of Christ's righteousness, you will not survive in a manner that pleases God. The foundational support against enemies that David discovered in God reminds us of the victory of God's people over Satan in Revelation 12:11 (NIV): "They triumphed over him by the blood of the Lamb and by the word of their testimony; they did not love their lives so much as to shrink from death." Unless the blood of the Lamb is your salvation, you will not survive the accusations Satan will make against you in the court of heaven. Unless the word of your testimony reflects a life conformed to God's Word, you will not survive the accusations of your own conscience. And unless you love him more than your own life, you will not survive an accusing world.

The Devil and His Accusations (vv. 1–3)

The most powerful accusations come from the devil to our consciences, often making us doubt the assurance of our salvation. We cannot hold up our record to silence his attacks. He will expose our hypocrisy every time. An appeal to the righteousness of Christ will be our only recourse. As David approaches God's house for worship, he must wonder, "Am I being accused in heaven's courts by the devil as Job was?" Like Job (29:11–18), David points to righteousness in his life. However, David ultimately appeals to the court of heaven and asks God to determine if there is evidence that divine love and truth have transformed his life. If there is such evidence, his life will, on the whole, be consistent and unwavering. In verse 1, the word translated "blameless" in the NIV (*tom*) signifies that no essential part of conduct is missing. It describes an overall pattern of righteous conformity to God's standards. God himself described David in this way, claiming that he walked before him in "integrity of heart and uprightness" (1 Kings 9:4, NIV). God knew David's record, so David could not be claiming his own righteousness but rather holding up evidence of God's love and truth working in his life.

Martin Luther struggled to gain assurance of his salvation for most of his life. The same vivid imagination which allowed him to preach and write with such color also worked against his confidence in grace at times:

> When I awoke last night, the Devil came and wanted to debate with me; he rebuked and reproached me, arguing that I was a sinner. To this I replied: Tell me something new, Devil! I already know that perfectly well; I have committed many a solid and real sin. Indeed there must be good honest sins—not fabricated and invented ones—for God to forgive for His beloved Son's sake, who took all my sins upon Him so that now the sins I have committed are no longer mine but belong to Christ. This wonderful gift of God I am not prepared to deny [in my response to the Devil], but want to acknowledge and confess.[1]

To discount the devil's accusations, we do not have to deny or conceal our sins; instead, like Luther did, we can acknowledge our sins, simultaneously acknowledging that we are forgiven in Christ. Only Christ can free us from the devil's accusations.

Our Conscience (vv. 4–7)

At other times, we will be accused by our own consciences, by memory of our past sins. To what do we appeal when that happens? While we are asking God to make his work obvious in our lives, we can also look for evidence in our lives that God's grace *has* been at work. We ask, "Are there attributes in my life that can only be explained by the grace of God?" David finds several that we should find as well.

First, the company we keep will confirm his work in us: "I do not sit with the deceitful, nor do I associate with hypocrites" (v. 4, NIV). This sounds similar to the way of the blessed person of Psalm 1. If you avoid the company of people who are deceitful, conniving, hypocritical, or slandering, you have good reason to believe that God is at work in you.

David presses further. Beyond outward disassociation, he notices that he has contempt for such company, saying, "I abhor the assembly of evildoers" (v. 5, NIV). Likewise, if you leave the company of people who constantly slander, criticize, or disdain biblical standards because you despise the profanation of God's holy name, then you have good reason that God is causing you to love what he loves and hate what he hates.

Finally, David notes the gift of a clean conscience, proclaiming, "I wash my hands in innocence, and go about your altar, LORD, proclaiming aloud your praise and telling of all your wonderful deeds" (vv. 6–7, NIV). In the Scriptures, "clean hands" is a metaphor for a sincere conscience (Isaiah 1:15; 33:15; 1 Timothy 2:8). Are you putting sin to death, not merely because you are afraid of public embarrassment but because you want to worship with all your might, unfettered by an accusing conscience? If you have spent your week cheating your customers, it will be impossible to delight in God's law. If you have spent your words in cutting down others, it will be impossible for you to sing, "I love thy church, O God." If you have spent your resources on self-gratification, it will be impossible to pray, "Take my life and let it be consecrated, Lord, to thee."[2]

David recognizes that he is aligning with God's company rather than God's enemies. Only a Christian has the ability to choose what pleases God, because Christ is renewing her will

(Romans 6; Galatians 2:20). Her ability to resolve with David ("I do not . . . nor do I," "I hate . . . and I will not") reveals God's work in her life.

Furthermore, David's expressions of personal hatred for God's enemies is instructive. Such anger does not *have* to be vindictive; and when it is not, it reveals a heart in line with God's. What makes you angry reveals the commitments of your heart. God demonstrates throughout the Bible that he is angered when his image-bearers are oppressed and plotted against. We see it most vividly in the book of Exodus when God goes to extraordinary lengths to deliver his people from their harsh slavery. If you are angered by plots against people, then you share the heart of God.

Throughout my ministry, I have had the privilege of working with many college students by virtue of my churches' college ministries. I have noticed a recurring theme as I talk with students who come to faith early in their college experience. When they return home during breaks from classes, their friends immediately notice a difference about them. The more they talk and catch up on their time away at college, the more opportunities these students have to share what Christ has done in their lives. While the Lord has sometimes used it to bring these friends to faith, it is more often the case that the friendship becomes distant. In other words, these new believers do not normally have to sever ties with old friends; ties fade away once they realize their lives are about following Christ.

The World (vv. 8–12)

Finally, opponents of Christianity will accuse us of hypocrisy. They will mock us as we seek to live in a way that is obedient to God. To what do we cling in the face of such accusation? David teaches us to cling to the love of Christ, saying, "LORD, I love the house where you live, the place where your glory dwells" (v. 8, NIV). One preacher called the love of Christ the "pole star" for godly living.[3] The pole star, or north star, is the reference point in the heavens for accurate navigation. By keeping your settings on that star, you will travel in the right direction. A similar thing is true in the Christian life. To maintain faith and obedience, one does not focus on keeping faith or keeping the commands. Instead, as we focus on Christ's love for us and our love for him, we will walk in the right direction.

There are two specific expressions of David's love in verses 8–10. First, David acknowledges that he loves to be in the presence of God. The "house" of God represented the presence of God in the Old Testament (v. 8). Second, David expresses love for God's ways (vv. 9–10). When you love someone, you want to be with him or her. If you love Christ, you will want to be in his presence. Of course, this means public worship, but not exclusively. You will desire to dwell in his presence continually. You will want to be near him in private devotions, in your thoughts during private moments, and at every moment of your workday. Of course, if you love him, you will especially want to be with him in eternity, because living on this side of the cross you desire to be near to the one who dared to draw near to you (John 1:14).

But how do you stir up a heart which has grown cold in its love for God? David provides an example in Psalm 18. "I love you, O Lord, my strength," he sings in verse 1, but verses 4–19 show us what provoked that love—God's moving heaven and earth to rescue him from spiritually drowning. Recalling the Lord's many acts of mercy in our past will rekindle our love.

Regarding his love for God's ways, David says that he is loyal in leading a blameless life because he loves God. He loves God because he knows him to be his merciful Redeemer. Leading a godly life is both an expression of loyalty and a confession of helplessness. In Psalm 119:134, David prays that God would redeem him *in order that he might obey.* Only love will pray a prayer like that. Selfishness prays for redemption in order to be spared of pain; love prays for redemption to please the beloved.

So how does a focus on the love of Christ's presence as well as on Christ's ways help in overcoming the accusations of the world? For one, we tend to compromise when we feel like we are alone. If we allow ourselves to believe that our self-worth is determined by the acceptance of another person or group, we place ourselves in danger. However, when we know that Christ has loved us enough to be with us, then we will be motivated to resist sins that would displease him.

In an article about hazing in fraternities and sororities, Hank Nuwr, a professor at Franklin College who has researched hazing, summarized the allure of Greek life despite its risks: "The collective need to belong is very, very strong."[4] Students are often willing to do things they never would have done because of the need to belong. In some tragic cases, students have died due to hazing and initiation and many of them live with regrets for the rest of their lives. Each of us has a need to belong, a need to be in the company of those who love us. Only Jesus can perfectly meet that need and has put on flesh to do so.

Secondly, the love of Christ is the only music loud enough to drown out the accusations of the world and call us to live obediently. A friend of mine says her husband's resolve to follow Christ despite her insults of his faith eventually conquered her. Immediately after coming to Christ, he began to attend church and take their little girl with him. With tears, she now says she would lounge by the pool on Sunday morning and wait for him to walk by. Then she would mock him, "There he goes, Mr. Goody Two Shoes! You take your little Bible and trot off to your stupid church!" It was not his rebukes that eventually melted her heart. It was his love for Christ regularly expressed in his life that defeated her unbelief. Your love for Christ will not only help you survive the world's attacks; it can enable you to subdue it.

"My feet stand on level ground," says David (Psalm 26:12, NIV). "[T]hey have conquered him by the blood of the Lamb and by the word of their testimony, for they loved not their lives even unto death," says John (Revelation 12:11). And Jesus says,

> [E]veryone who hears these words of mine and puts them into practice is like a wise man who built his house on the rock. The rain came down, the streams rose, and the winds blew and beat against that house; yet it did not fall, because it had its foundation on the rock. But everyone who hears these words of mine and does not put them into practice is like a foolish man who built his house on sand. The rain came down, the streams rose, and the winds blew and beat against that house, and it fell with a great crash. (Matthew 7:24–27, NIV)

What will it be? Will you build your life on the rock or on a sham? Will your life survive the storm of accusation from the devil, your own conscience, and the world? Or will it fall with a great crash? Build your life on the rock, Jesus Christ, and you will never be put to shame.

Questions for Reflection/Discussion

1. Which category of accusation (the devil, conscience, the world) can you relate with the most? Why?

2. What firm foundation to sustain you was revealed to you in this chapter?

3. Is there a verse or verses in this psalm that remind you of that firm foundation? If so, consider committing that scripture to memory so that the Spirit can use it to give you assurance and peace when you are accused.

Prayer

Where are you facing accusation right now, whether externally or internally? Lift your concerns up to God, remembering that Christ has taken your accusations upon himself. Consider also how to walk as one who is free from guilt, keeping the steadfast love of the Lord before your eyes (v.3), avoiding the influence of the godless (vv. 4–5), and standing on the level ground of his work on your behalf (v.12). Thank God that Jesus has freed you from the weighty burden of guilt and shame.

10

Waiting Confidently

Psalm 27

Wait for the LORD; be strong,
and let your heart take courage; wait for the LORD!
(Psalm 27:14)

PSALM 26 SHOWED us the firm foundation of Christ's righteousness. Psalm 27 lifts up our eyes toward the hope of deliverance as we stand secure in Christ. It enables us to wait on the Lord's
timing, not in anxious uncertainty but in confident expectation.

Sometimes it is hard to believe liberation from this fallen
world will ever come. Enslaved people can become so traumatized they find freedom too good to be true. Abraham Lincoln's
Emancipation Proclamation banned slavery in America. Across
the South, headlines read, "Slavery Legally Abolished." Despite
it, the vast majority of slaves in the South never left their masters.
Fellow Memphian Shelby Foote wrote of this strange phenomenon, "[E]very slave could repeat with equal validity, what an
Alabama slave had said in 1864 when asked what he thought of
the Great Emancipator whose proclamation went into effect that
year: 'I don't know nothin' bout Abraham Lincoln,' he replied,
'cep they say he set us free. And I don't know nothin' bout that
neither.'"[1] (Of course, we must also acknowledge the lack of

resources available to slaves to support themselves if they did leave their slavery. This fear likely also contributed to their reservations about leaving their slavery.)

In this psalm, David is longing for liberation. While the exact circumstances surrounding this psalm are unknown, it is clear David is emotionally affected due to the repeated reference to his heart. While he is in this emotional turmoil, he waits in defiant hope for emancipation. He does so because his hope is in the Lord. Because God has been his helper in the past, he knows that God is worth waiting for.

Who are your enemies? What do you do when you're surrounded by them? They may be real people who want to destroy your career. They may be worries about the future. They may be besetting sins. They may be cultural forces like school and workplace violence, abortion, or secularism. If God is your God, you do not have to be overwhelmed by them. You can perch yourself on a hill and wait for God to deliver you. In this passage, the Lord compels us to wait confidently in this life.

David recognizes that God's attributes precisely match his needs (vv. 1–3). In contrast to the dark deeds of adversaries who try to trap and harm him, God is his "light," his "salvation," and his "stronghold" (v. 1) so that even when his adversaries seek to do him harm (vv. 2–3), "even then will [he] be confident" (v. 3, NIV). Every characteristic of God revealed in Scripture fulfills a need we have in redemption. He is revealed as holy, because in a world filled with sin we need a source of purity. He is revealed as all-powerful, because it takes supreme power to rescue us from our enemies. He is revealed as everywhere present, because his people all over the world need him to be near.

God Is Our Salvation

David's most obvious need is deliverance from human enemies. His mockers accuse him of hypocrisy, and surrounding nations are envious of his position. Some apparently are "advanc[ing] against [him] to devour [him]" (v. 2, NIV). David needs a real-life deliverer. The history of David's life demonstrates that God delivered him frequently from earthly enemies (1 Samuel 19–31; 2 Samuel 5–10). God gave David *earthly* rescue to prove that, more importantly, he was David's *spiritual* Savior.

Furthermore, God delivered David in order to deliver *us*. If David had been destroyed, the line of Jesus would have been stopped and there would have been no Savior. If there had been no Savior, we would have been left in the self-destruction of our sin and received hell as our just punishment. God was David's salvation so that Jesus could become ours. We need salvation. God *is* salvation.

God Is Our Refuge

God is not only our salvation; he is also our "stronghold," or refuge (v. 1b). It is possible to be delivered from physical danger and still be emotionally scarred. A person could be saved from a burning building but remain traumatized, and fearful of the memories of the event. For patients receiving chemotherapy, treatment can at times be so miserable that the cure seems worse than the disease.

David finds not only a deliverer in God, but an emotional refuge. At the end of verse 1 and beginning of verse 3, David says he will not be afraid because God is his stronghold. God is so gracious that he not only attends to our need for salvation, but also ministers to our emotional need for assurance. We find the same truth in the New Testament: "[D]o not be anxious about anything, but in everything by prayer and supplication with thanksgiving let your requests be made known to God. And the peace of God, which surpasses all understanding, will guard [military imagery] your hearts and your minds in Christ Jesus" (Philippians 4:6–7). We need an emotional refuge. God is our stronghold.

God Is Our Light

God is also "light" (v. 1a). While God is often associated with light (Job 38:19; Psalm 36:9; 104:2), this is the only place in the Old Testament where he is actually *called* light. In the New Testament, there are several direct references to God as our light. This comes to expression particularly in the presentation of Jesus, who said, "I am the light of the world. Whoever follows me will not walk in darkness but will have the light of life" (John 8:12). This light works *against* the darkness: "The light shines in the darkness, but the darkness has not understood it" (John 1:5, NIRV). In John's first epistle the identification of Jesus with God is clear as God himself is referred to as light: "God is light; in him there is no darkness at all" (1 John 1:5, NIV). The image of light in the Bible refers to more than one thing. Sometimes it refers to truth (Psalm 43:3), sometimes to goodness (Isaiah 5:20), sometimes to joy (Psalm 97:11), and sometimes vitality (Psalm 36:9). But it always refers to the power of God over and against the various forms of darkness in the world.

Of course, God is not literally light. But the mysterious and multifaceted powers of light give us insight into this psalm. God is everything we need. David says that God is light first because every attribute that follows is an aspect of this fundamental conviction. As our light, he is our truth, goodness, joy, vitality, salvation, and stronghold. The opposite of having God's light is to live in darkness and to have none of these good things. That is why David's enemies will "stumble and fall" (v. 2). But to know that God is your light is to know that God is with you to provide everything you need, so that you can wait confidently for his relief.

God's Church

As David looks around him, he sees another reason to wait confidently for God's deliverance; he is surrounded by the people of God:

> One thing I ask from the LORD,
>   this only do I seek:
> that I may dwell in the house of the LORD
>   all the days of my life,
> to gaze on the beauty of the LORD
>   and to seek him in his temple.
> For in the day of trouble
>   he will keep me safe in his dwelling;
> he will hide me in the shelter of his sacred tent
>   and set me high upon a rock.
> Then my head will be exalted
>   above the enemies who surround me;
> at his sacred tent I will sacrifice with shouts of joy;
>   I will sing and make music to the LORD. (vv. 4–6,
>   NIV)

Many years ago, I read an article that made a major impact on the way I think about corporate worship. The pastor's point was that we should be aware that pastoral care is occurring in the midst of worship. In the midst of the worship service, people are being put back together. A young professional terrified of the future is being comforted as he sings, "Father, I know that all my life is portioned out for me." A mother who grew up in a dysfunctional home is learning how to train up her children in love as she watches an older mother and her daughter worship together. An addict is beginning to understand that he is not left to his own resources to find freedom. A beaten-up public leader basks in the unconditional love of his brothers and sisters in Christ.[2]

That article caught my attention, because at the time I was ministering to the most confused, conflicted, and degraded man I had ever met in my life. He had come to Christ and was desperate to be set free from his sins and healed of his pathologies. He would come to worship late and leave early because he couldn't bear to speak with anyone. To be free of distractions, he would often sit in the cry room (my little church didn't have many babies then!). He said those were the only sane moments of his week.

Something real happens when God's people are gathered in God's house to worship—something that cannot happen by video or audio or in your personal quiet time. The Puritan Richard Sibbes said, "Particular visible churches under visible pastors . . . now are God's tabernacle."[3] It reminds us that we do not come to worship just for ourselves; we come for each other. Hebrews 10:25 (NIV1984) instructs that we must not "give up meeting together, as some are in the habit of doing, but let us encourage one another."

There are three aspects of corporate worship that David finds beneficial in his time of distress. For one, worship should be the experience of God's beauty in contrast to a world made ugly by selfish attitudes, violence, and pain. Every reasonable effort should be given to make any place God's people gather for worship beautiful. We are embodied souls, so our physical environment shapes the way we think and feel. We gather in worship to gaze on the "fair beauty of the Lord" with spiritual eyes, but our physical senses will either be aided in that pursuit or distracted by our setting.[4]

We also recognize in corporate worship that we are not alone. There is safety in numbers. Elijah was distressed until God told him that there were seven thousand in Israel who still worshiped God (cf. 1 Kings 19:3–9; Romans 11:2–5). In Psalm 22 David is "in the midst of the congregation" (v. 22) and finds shelter. When you come together with other people on Sunday morning, you should be reminded that you have a shelter that others wish they had. It is painful to watch those who don't know God and don't worship with his people grieve a tragedy all by themselves, welcome a new baby just to their own home, endure a physical trauma without the prayers of God's people, or worry because their kids don't have good friends. There is safety in God's house. In God's house, we can experience "joy" (v. 6). You will find little reason to rejoice if television, social media, or the daily news are your only diet. It will be in corporate worship that your perspective is realigned.

Like David, the psalmist Asaph knew that to be true. On one occasion, he was distressed that the wicked prospered while the righteous struggled. That is, until he "entered the sanctuary of God" (Psalm 73:17, NIV). Then his attitude was realigned because he "understood their final destiny" (v. 17). They would be "cast . . . down to ruin . . . destroyed, completely swept away by terrors!" (vv. 18–19).

After a week of news about terrorist attacks, it is in worship that you joyfully remember that this world is not your home. After a week of feeling like you are the only Christian in your school, it is in worship that you joyfully realize you are not alone. After a week of criticism from a relative, it is in worship that you can joyfully hear God's sweet words of grace to you. After a week of confusion over the future, it is in worship that you can joyfully refocus on the God who is sovereign over all your life. Through the gift of corporate worship, God will enable you to "sacrifice with shouts of joy" and "sing and make music to the LORD" (Psalm 27:6).

God Is Our Father

Finally, David is encouraged to wait confidently for his deliverance because his God is a heavenly Father: "For my father and my mother have forsaken me, but the LORD will take me in" (v. 10). David says that even if the unlikely should occur—that his parents would forsake him—God will not. The Lord is the perfect

Father. One finds in this Father alone what every child seeks from his parents.

Every child desires to be listened to. David expresses that same desire in this psalm, saying, "Hear my voice when I call, LORD" (v. 7, NIV). Children sometimes talk just to be heard rather than to be instructed. Children need to experience the exchange of ideas rather than merely engage in functional language (i.e., "Did you get your homework done?" "Where are you going?" "Clean your room."). It is this loving Father's face toward David that moves David to seek his face in return. God desires for us to come to him. David cries out to God, because he knows that his Father delights in the conversation.

David also expresses every child's desire to be accepted by her mom and dad: "Do not hide your face from me" (v. 9, NIV). Few things are more devastating to children, even adult children, as when their parents reject their ideas, vocation, physical appearance, or spouse. Because God is a perfect Father and has been reconciled to us in Jesus Christ, we may be assured that though everyone else rejects us, he accepts us.

Children need guidance; they don't naturally know how to make it through life. Likewise, we don't know how to live in this complicated world on our own. We need to be guided. David encourages us to go to our Father for guidance, saying "Teach me your way, LORD; lead me in a straight path" (v. 11, NIV).

Finally, children need their parents' protection: "Do not turn me over to the desire of my foes" (v. 12, NIV). God never tells us to be self-sufficient. Instead, he commands us to be courageous because he is with us. That can be hard for us to hear. One time a widow asked me to speak on Joshua 1:6–9 at her husband's funeral. So I urged the family to be strong and courageous, but emphasized that those words were surrounded by God's promise to be with them like loving arms around a child. In other words, only the presence of God can produce strength and courage in us. When I got back to the office, there was already a message waiting for me from someone who had attended the funeral. She was irate that I had urged this family to be strong in the midst of their grief. She hadn't heard the promises. You must be willing to become a child and let God protect you.

When weighed down by life's circumstances, God reminds us by his word that we should be encouraged to wait patiently for his deliverance. He is our salvation. He is our refuge. He is light that overcomes all darkness. He gives us a place in his church in order to strengthen and encourage us throughout this life. And he is our perfect Father who will one day deliver us from all evil.

Questions for Reflection/Discussion

1. Does waiting feel counterintuitive to you? Why so?

2. What hope does God give you in this psalm to enable you to wait confidently rather than anxiously?

3 How does God use other people in the church to give us hope? How might you make use of God's blessing of the church to give you hope?

Prayer

Where are you finding it difficult to wait right now? Pray through this psalm in your own words, acknowledging the way God meets all of your needs as described in the psalm:

- He is your light and your salvation (v. 1).
- He is the stronghold of your life (v. 2).
- You can be confident in the midst of oppression (v. 3).
- He will hide you in his shelter in your day of trouble (v. 5)
- He will not forsake you (v. 10).
- You will see his goodness (v. 13).

Ask the Lord to enable you to wait with hope and give you joy as you consider these truths.

11

Thy Kingdom Come

Psalm 35

You have seen, O LORD; be not silent!
O Lord, be not far from me!
(Psalm 35:22)

PSALM 35 CAN help to free us from self-focus. You may not immediately know why you would want to be freed from self-focus. We like to focus on ourselves, after all. However, notice the progression of thought here. Psalm 27 enables us to lift our eyes up from our own circumstances because of the beautiful reality of liberation. This psalm shows us that when we focus on Christ and give over every part of our lives to his kingdom, we see ourselves as a precious part of his kingdom and therefore pray that his will, not ours, would be done. This actually increases our boldness in prayer and therefore our hope in God.

On one occasion I was seated next to a Christian Scientist at a wedding reception. I had performed the ceremony, and later the bride and groom admitted to arranging the seating so that I could interact with this particular person. As the conversation progressed, this very pleasant woman emphasized how similar our churches were. "Like you," she said, "we read the Scriptures and we admire Jesus."

Remembering that Harry Ironside had a similar conversation with a Christian Scientist who came into his bookshop in

Oakland, I decided to focus the discussion in the same way he did.[1] So I asked, "Do you believe the Scriptures?"

"Yes!" she exclaimed, "We read them at every service and then cross-reference them to Mary Baker Eddy's *Science and Health*."

"Ah good," I continued, "so you agree with the Bible when it says that the blood of Jesus is 'precious' (1 Peter 1:19)?"

This question certainly focused the discussion. While she did not turn red in the face, bang her fist on the table, and blaspheme, "The blood of Jesus is no more to me than the blood of any other dead Jew," as Ironside's patron did, she was clearly offended by the concept. She had been well trained to despise the concept that Jesus died to atone for sin. The remainder of our conversation was cordial, but the question opened the door to share with her how much more beautiful the Bible's story of a Christ who saves is than Eddy's revised account of a Jesus who stands only as a moral and religious example. Jesus, as we will see, is much more than a moral example; his life is woven into the fabric of the Psalter so that it becomes not only the paradigm but the very source of our life in God.

The book of Psalms comprises various genres like petition, thanksgiving, and penance. Psalm 35 is an example of an imprecatory psalm, that is, a prayer that calls down judgment on the enemies of God. Some say that such a prayer is "a cry unsuited to the church."[2] Some readily dismiss these psalms because they do not believe the Bible is inspired by God. For instance, John J. Owen (not the Puritan) says contemptuously, "[these] forms of expression are of such cold-blooded and malignant cruelty, as to preclude entertaining the idea for a moment that they were inspired of God"[3] However, there are others who take the Bible seriously but say imprecatory psalms are inspired as examples to be rejected. For instance, Peter Craigie condemns these prayers as "in themselves evil."[4]

But we must believe what the Bible says of itself: "All Scripture is God-breathed" (2 Timothy 3:16, NIV). Furthermore, the Bible teaches that what David wrote was divinely inspired (2 Samuel 23:1–2; Mark 12:36; Acts 1:16). The New Testament makes it clear that we are to pray against God's enemies after the cross, just as we were called to do while anticipating the cross.[5] For instance, Jesus pronounced seven woes upon the scribes and Pharisees (Matthew 23:13–35). Paul, the preacher of grace, said: "If anyone does not love the Lord, a curse be on him" (1 Corinthians 16:22, HCSB). And about those who were trying to add works to the gospel, he exclaimed, "Let him be accursed" (Galatians 1:8, KJV).

Through the ages, the church has believed that Jesus spoke the words of the psalms as his own. Men like Augustine, Jerome, Ambrose, Arnobius, Cassiodorus, Hilary, Prosper, and Tertullian all viewed the Psalms as the prayers of Christ.[6] The modern church has believed the same. George Horne, the eighteenth-century Bishop of Norwich and Spurgeon's favorite commentator on the Psalms, said that in the Psalms we have the words of Christ as he becomes sin for us.[7] Ernst Hengstenberg, in the 1800s, said that these imprecatory psalms are worthy of Christ because they were "spoken by him."[8]

For example, Jesus adopted the words of Psalm 41:8–10 as his own pronouncement of judgment on Judas (Matthew 26:23–24). As we have seen previously, from the cross he cried, "My God, my God, why have you forsaken me?" as his own words (Psalm 22:1; Matthew 27:46). And later he prayed, "Into your hands I commit my spirit" (Psalm 31:5; Luke 23:46). Jesus was not merely quoting poetry; he was speaking these words as his very own. They had always been his words, first spoken through David, now spoken with his own lips.

The author of Hebrews also affirmed that the Psalms were spoken by Christ through David. The writer says, "So Jesus is not ashamed to call them brothers and sisters" (Hebrews 2:11–12, NIV), then quotes Psalm 22:22. Nowhere in the Gospels is it recorded that Jesus spoke those words in his earthly ministry. Later in Hebrews 10:5 (NIV), the author says, "Therefore when

Christ came into the world, he said. . ." and the quote that follows is from Psalm 40:6–8. Again, the Gospels don't record it, but the author of Hebrews recognized that Christ was speaking these words in the Psalms whether or not he pronounced them during the days of his life on earth.

So, if these are Christ's words, what do they express? They reveal his desire that his kingdom, his rule over all people and institutions, would come to expression. That calls us to submit our wills to the same purpose. It calls on us to love him so passionately, to consider him so precious, that we make the coming of his kingdom our greatest aim.

On a cultural level, we must pray that his kingdom would be made known in reformed government, decreased crime, human concern in business, eradication of abortion, racism, sexism, child abuse, removal of gambling, cure of poverty and diseases, and so forth. On a personal level, we must pray that churches would flourish, biblical principles would reign in our lives, prayer would become more consistent in our lives, our families would reflect grace, and so forth. We desire these things not for our comfort or betterment; we desire them because we love Christ and recognize that these are the manifestations of his kingdom that he desires.

Not only must we make his desires our desires, but also his words our words. Knowing what we know now, we read these words as Christ's and therefore pray them as Christ's, *not ours* (vv. 1–18). David is praying for his enemies to be defeated so that the progress of his kingdom would not be interrupted. While it is clear that we must not dismiss these portions of Scripture, the Bible also makes it clear that we must not pray them as our own words of vengeance. We have one duty toward our enemies and that is to love them:

> Do not repay anyone evil for evil. Be careful to do what is
> right in the eyes of everybody. If it is possible, as far as it
> depends on you, live at peace with everyone. Do not take

revenge, my friends, but leave room for God's wrath, for it is written: "It is mine to avenge; I will repay," says the Lord. On the contrary:

"If your enemy is hungry, feed him; if he is thirsty, give him something to drink. In doing this, you will heap burning coals on his head." (Romans 12:17–21, NIV)

Put more simply by Jesus in Matthew 5:44 (NIV), "But I tell you, love your enemies and pray for those who persecute you." So how do we pray these words of Christ and not make them our own words of vengeance? We pray that *Christ's* enemies will be defeated, rather than our personal ones. We surrender our rights of revenge to him and allow him to decide if our enemies are his or not. Perhaps they are ours by our own making. Or perhaps they are not really enemies, simply those who disagree with us over issues that are eternally inconsequential. Perhaps they are even agents of God's grace who keep us from doing that which is foolish. Surrendering all vengeance to Christ means that we are even prepared to suffer peacefully at the hands of those who seem to be our enemies, if that is what Christ chooses.

Finally, we understand from this psalm that we have the privilege of praying fervently that all of Christ's enemies would be conquered first by conversion. The goal of God's judgment is always conversion. God makes it clear that if he pronounces judgment on a people and they repent, he will relent of his judgment (Jeremiah 18:7–9). If repentance does not occur, then of course, God's judgment proceeds (Jeremiah 18:10-11).

So in Psalm 35, Christ prays that his enemies would be put to shame and confusion and be clothed in shame and disgrace *if they don't repent* (v. 25). In contrast to verse 25, verse 27 is in part a description of what he desires for his enemies to say: "Great is the LORD, who delights in the welfare of his servant!" This prayer was answered when the centurion who presided over Christ's death later concluded, "Surely he was the Son of God!"

(Matthew 27:54, NIV). And it was answered when Saul was stricken blind and transformed from a persecutor of Christ into an apostle (Acts 22:7).

In more recent history, we find examples of effective prayers for the conversion of those outside God's family. For instance, for years, Afghanistan's borders were closed to the gospel. But when the Soviets invaded Afghanistan, many Afghans were forced to flee to refugee camps outside their borders. Many heard the good news and were converted to Christ, and when they returned they took the gospel with them.

War is always a horrible evil, and Afghans have suffered unspeakably as their land has been used for numerous proxy wars. But even in unimaginably tragic situations like wars and pogroms—the raging of the kings of the earth (cf. Psalm 2:1–2)—God secretly works his redemptive purposes. Ultimately, we should pray for Christ's enemies to be conquered by conversion.

In his theological work *Doxology,* Geoffrey Wainwright tells the story of an Armenian family captured by Turks. After looting an Armenian home, a Turkish officer killed the elderly parents and gave the daughters to his soldiers. But the oldest daughter he kept for himself. Amazingly, she escaped his bondage and trained to be a nurse. Afterward, she was assigned to a hospital treating Turkish officers. One evening her lantern illumined the face of the monster who had kept her in bondage. When the Turkish officer recovered, the doctor explained to him, "But for her devotion to you, you would be dead."

The officer looked at the face of the nurse, who was standing nearby, and said, "We have met before, haven't we?"

"Yes," she said, "We have met before."

"Why didn't you kill me?" he asked.

Her answer was, "I am a follower of him who said, 'Love your enemies.'"[9]

This woman had obviously abandoned revenge to God such that she was ready to show love. And though we know nothing of the conversion of the officer, we know that good conquered evil because the story would have never been told if she had stabbed him in the chest. Christ's kingdom is precious. We should pray, like Christ, that its opponents would be overcome by the only love that can withhold judgment from those who repent.

Questions for Reflection/Discussion

1. How does reading the Psalms as the words of Jesus inform your understanding of the Psalms in general? What about imprecatory psalms, specifically?

2. The forces of evil that cause so much of our suffering, anxiety, etc., are prayed against by Jesus in this psalm. How does this give us comfort?

3. How does Jesus's love for us, who were once his enemies, help us to pray these types of prayers in a righteous rather than a selfish way?

Prayer

Use this psalm as a guide to show you how to pray that God's will would be done in situations where others are causing harm. Pray for them to be captured and changed by God's grace, rather than suffer the consequences of unrepentance. At the end of your prayer, ask God to give you a hopeful attitude about the situation, because he is at work in it. Ask for clarity about where to be a light of truth and hope as he guides you.

12

When Life Gets to You

Psalm 37

Delight yourself in the LORD,
and he will give you the desires of your heart.
(Psalm 37:4)

IN THE PREVIOUS chapter, we saw that the Psalter expresses a longing for God's coming kingdom. Praying for God's kingdom sometimes involves asking God to exercise his judgment on the wicked, as we see modeled in Psalm 35. In a similar vein, Psalm 37 begins with a promise about the evildoers Psalm 35 instructs us to pray against: "they will soon fade like the grass" (v. 2). However, we may still experience emotional turmoil because of their evil deeds. Psalm 37 shows us what to do in the meantime.

The benefit of having a whole Bible rather than just one testament is that you have both testaments to comment on each other. While we usually think of the New Testament enlightening the Old, this psalm serves as a commentary on the third beatitude, "Blessed are the meek, for they will inherit the earth" (Matthew 5:5).

Leaving justice in the hands of God may not feel like strength. In fact, it may feel like weakness. However, meekness is not weakness. The Bible teaches that meekness is strength, derived from trust in a sovereign God. Nicholas Wolterstorff quotes a seventeenth-century writer to make this point: "I had rather see coming toward me a whole regiment with drawn swords, than one lone Calvinist convinced that he is doing the will of God."[1] A Calvinist is one who believes God is absolutely sovereign. Thomas Case exemplified such confidence in God's sovereignty that he took on the reform of social structures, saying to the English House of Commons in 1641:

> Reformation must be universal . . . reform all places, all persons and all callings; reform the benches of judgment . . . reform the universities, reform the cities, reform the countries . . . reform the Sabbath, reform the ordinances, the worship of God . . . you have more work to do than I can speak. . . . Every plant which my heavenly father hath not planted shall be rooted up.[2]

Because God is sovereign, those of us who trust him are free from the burden to work up our courage when life gets to us. Instead, we can derive our strength from trusting in a sovereign Father and fearlessly seeking first his kingdom.

David outlines several specific ways we can put our trust in God. The first step is to quiet our spirits when we are angry about the wicked (vv. 1–11). Though the NIV says "do not fret" in verses 1, 7, and 8, the text literally says, "Don't get heated." Human anger does not accomplish God's purposes (James 1:20; cf. Romans 12:21). You will never defeat evil by getting angry. Instead of succumbing to anger, we are called to redirect our eyes to the Lord. In short, this psalm calls us to look up and look ahead.

Look Up

Verse 3 (NIV) says, "Trust in the Lord and do good; dwell in the land and enjoy safe pasture." Don't get overwhelmed with all the evil around the world. Focus on dealing with it in your pasture— primarily your heart, your home, and your vocation.

David then commands us, "Delight yourself in the LORD"—that is, make him our primary desire (v. 4). Delighting in God requires spending time with him. That occurs in weekly worship, morning and evening, but it also occurs by spending time with him regularly throughout the week. We may get incensed by the headlines we read in the morning, livid at the news show we hear at noon, and frustrated at someone who wrongs us at work. But we can also press against cynicism and hopelessness by pausing to pray, taking a few minutes to read Scripture, and thanking God for his fatherly care in the midst of times in which, like the psalmist, "There are many who say, 'Who will show us some good?'" (Psalm 4:6). If we can learn, with David, the practice of looking up to God in the midst of our troubles, we will find our confidence strengthened and our hope kindled.

Look Ahead

We must not only look up; we must also look ahead. "Commit your way to the LORD"—or more literally, "roll your way on him" (v. 5). God allows us to roll our burdens onto him rather than trying to carry them by ourselves. Each of us is concerned about our future, our career, our security, and our reputation. "What if I get sick? Or someone steals my pension? Or an enemy falsely accuses me? Or my children turn away from God and me?" The Father invites us to roll those worries on him. In return, he promises to vindicate you. That is certainly a promise for the great day of God's future judgment, but it is also true that the rightness of your ways will be made clear in this life: "[T]rust in him, and he will act. He will bring forth your righteousness as the light, and your justice as the noonday" (vv. 5–6).

Held vs. Held Up

The last three-quarters of the psalm urge us to contrast two paths when we feel helpless before the wicked. First, the righteous will be *upheld* but the wicked will be *held up* (vv. 12–17, 23–24). The wicked have no lasting power against the righteous. While enemies may secretly plot their strategies, God knows their plans and laughs because he knows he will destroy them eventually (vv. 12–13). God promises to avenge whatever actions are taken against his people when he returns (vv. 14–15; cf. 2 Thessalonians 1:6–10). Finally, he assures us that though God's people may have very little money, they have all power because they are upheld by God. It doesn't matter what plots are made against you, how powerful and numerous the weapons pointed at you are, or how few resources you have, as a child of God, you are secure in both this life and the one to come.

God orders the course of your life in such a way that you will accomplish eternally significant things (vv. 23–24). The Lord guides your life, making your steps firm even when there is stumbling along the way: "though he may stumble, he will not fall" (v. 24, NIV). This is by God's design. We may stumble, but he will keep us from falling to our eternal ruin, "for the LORD upholds him with his hand" (v. 24, NIV). In his biography of George Müller, A. T. Pierson quotes this verse, "The steps of the good man are ordered by the Lord." Then he adds, "Yes, and the *stops* too."[3] Sometimes in order to accomplish his purpose for us, God must put us flat on our backs or stop us dead in our tracks. Those are not times of failure but enforced periods of rest and waiting given to us by God to refocus on him.

Known vs. Ignored

Second, the righteous are known but the wicked are ignored (vv. 18–20). As in English, the Hebrew word translated "to know" conveys intimacy. God does not merely recognize you; he knows you thoroughly. The Bible uses this word to describe the intimate relations between a husband and wife: "Adam *knew* Eve . . . and she conceived" (Genesis 4:1, emphasis added). It is even used to describe the foreordaining knowledge that God had about us before we were born. Of Jeremiah he said, "Before I formed you in the womb I *knew* you" (Jeremiah 1:5, emphasis added).

In this psalm, God says he intimately cares for us, which explains why "disaster" and "famine" cannot destroy us and why our "inheritance will endure forever" (v. 18–19, NIV). The unbeliever's lot is sad in contrast. God does not know him in the same way (cf. Psalm 1:4, 6). Yes, God knows everything he is doing, but he does not take a caring part in that person's life. He is, as it were, all alone.

Give vs. Grab

Third, the righteous give but the wicked grab: "The wicked borrow and do not repay, but the righteous give generously" (vv. 21–22, NIV). Greed is one of the ugliest of sins. Recently, I watched a documentary on the purchase of life insurance policies. One couple purchased policies on twelve AIDS patients who were expected to die within two years. But when new and more powerful drugs were introduced, the lives of these patients were extended—and the couple became angry that the patients were not dying. What a miserable life greed leads to!

Greed can be more subtle as well, but it makes us just as miserable. Some people avoid investing in the kingdom of God because they are busy spending everything they have on themselves—new cars, new things for the house, electronic toys, expensive vacations, excessive eating out, etc. Greed, the unwillingness to wait on something desired, leads many into heavy debt, so any extra income goes to pay off credit cards. Some never practice hospitality because they don't want anyone to mess up their house or disturb their schedule.

Joyful generosity characterizes Christians who know that Jesus is their king. The righteous are described with this simple line: they "give generously" (v. 21, NIV). It is a blessing to live a generous life. Paul says that even God is blessed by our giving, because those who benefit from it thank him (2 Corinthians 9:12). People are also blessed when we give: their "hearts will go out to [us]" (2 Corinthians 9:14, NIV), and their needs will be met. And, as Jesus said, being a blessing to others is itself a blessing: "It is more blessed to give than to receive" (Acts 20:35, NIV). It is a blessing to bond with missionaries and ministers whom you support financially, and it is a delight to discover a need that a brother or sister has and to help supply it. A generous life is one God gives to a believer who delights to respond to the grace of Jesus (2 Corinthians 8:9).

The Long View

In the final verses of the psalm, the psalmist urges us to take a long view of things when we are envious of the wicked (vv. 25–40). We seldom have an accurate perspective when we look only at the immediate. Those who lead powerful lives are those who trust God for the long haul and invest their lives accordingly. The psalmist calls us to a long view in three areas: children, obedience, and life's problems.

Children

David's assurance the children of the righteous "will be a blessing" (v. 26) is a reminder to instill kingdom values in them. That is an exhortation to every member of the church, not just parents. One of the chief purposes of a congregation is to pass its faith on to the next generation.

I view myself as a children's minister. I preach to many children every week in the sanctuary, but I am also preaching to many adults, urging them week by week to keep a vow they make at every child's baptism: "Will you order your lives in such a way that you will not cause this little one to stumble?" Investing in children is among the most important work we can do in the church. It can be difficult work, with little to no recognition or immediately evident results. However, it is absolutely worth doing, because by it we raise up the next generation of our church to be faithful followers of Jesus.

Obedience

In verses 27–36 David calls us to a long view of obedience, recounting several promises: the righteous will "dwell in the land forever" (v. 27, NIV); God "will exalt you to inherit the land" and see the destruction of the wicked (v. 34, NIV); the "wicked and ruthless man" will "soon [pass] away" and be no more (vv. 35–36, NIV). Conforming to biblical principles may not seem practical or profitable at the moment. It may set you back financially to pay someone what you owe them. To refuse to do something that is illegal may draw derision from onlookers. You might even feel like a fool for not engaging in a practice that is making others rich. But this psalm gives us the promises that enable us to keep the long view.

Moral shortcuts may seem expedient for the moment, but God always puts an end to them—sometimes in this life but certainly in the one to come. We are enabled to "swim upstream" against the predominant culture when God puts his law in our hearts. David illustrates the outcome—the believer's desires become like his Lord's:

Take delight in the LORD,
    and he will give you the desires of your heart.
Commit your way to the LORD;
    trust in him and he will do this:
He will make your righteous reward shine like the dawn,
    your vindication like the noonday sun. (vv. 4–6,
        NIV; cf. 27–31)

These promises are not found only in this psalm. In Matthew 6:33 (NIV) Jesus calls those who follow him to "seek first his kingdom and his righteousness, and all these things will be given to you as well." In perhaps an even more tangible demonstration of this reality, Hebrews 11:7 (NIV) explains how Noah's obedience was ultimately for the best for he and his family: "By faith Noah, when warned about things not yet seen, in holy fear built an ark to save his family. By his faith he condemned the world and became heir of the righteousness that is in keeping with faith."

Through numerous examples in his Word, God demonstrates why it is to our benefit to take a long view of obedience. We are not saved by our obedience, but God has promised us that it will go well with us when we live life in accord with the way he designed it (cf. Deuteronomy 12:28).

Life's Problems

Finally, we are called to keep a long view of all of life's problems (vv. 37–40). However burdensome they are for the moment, the Bible says that they are "light and momentary" in comparison to the weight of glory we will experience (2 Corinthians 4:17, NIV). Harry Ironside has this poignant line: "All the heaven the [wicked] are ever going to know they get in this world, and all the trouble God's saints will know they are getting here."[4]

Trusting God to bring justice on all evil is ultimately founded on the personal price he has paid to justify us and make us his righteous people. We can rely on him to be a "stronghold in time of trouble" (v. 39, NIV), because the one who is "just" proved himself the "one who justifies those who have faith in Jesus" whom "God presented as a sacrifice of atonement through faith in his blood" (Romans 3:25–26, NIV). By the cross, God proved infallibly he "delivers [us] from the wicked and saves [us]" forever (v. 40, NIV).

Questions for Reflection/Discussion

1. What hope does this psalm give to us when we "look up"?

2. What similarities do you see between the two paths described in this psalm and in Psalm 1? How does Jesus lead us in the righteous path in this psalm just as he did in Psalm 1?

3. In which category—children, obedience, life's problems—is it most difficult for you to keep a "long view"? What promise(s) does this psalm provide to help you in this?

Prayer

Recall the situation in which you asked for God's will to be done in the previous chapter. Then, pray through this psalm, asking God to enable you to trust in him and to faithfully do good in the middle of the situation (v.3). More than that, ask him to give you the "delight" this psalm speaks of despite the way your circumstances might make you feel, and to help you identify ways to turn your attention to how you can bless others and trust in his justice.

13

Life under Heaven

Psalm 49

Truly no man can ransom another,
or give to God the price of his life.
(Psalm 49:7)

IN 1518 MARTIN Luther was interrogated by Cardinal Cajetan at Augsburg. Through the cardinal, the pope was trying to force Luther to recant his belief that a person is justified before a holy God by receiving the gift of Christ's righteousness by faith. When the cardinal first saw Luther, he mocked the monk's appearance: "That brother has deep eyes and so must have strange fancies in his head." Then an Italian representing the cardinal was sent to Luther to pressure him into denying his faith. He said, "Only utter this one word, *revoco*, and the cardinal will commend you to the pope and you shall return with glory to your elector." Despite the pressure, Luther refused, so the incensed cardinal thundered at the impudent monk, trying to intimidate him with the pope's political and material power:

> "What do you think the pope cares for Germany? Do you think the princes will defend you by arms?"
>
> "No," said Luther.
>
> "Then where will you live?" asked the cardinal.
>
> Luther's answer is one of the great examples of Christian heroism: "Under heaven," he replied.[1]

One of the challenges of the Christian life is rightly viewing material possessions. We know we must have certain things in order to live, but we also know that "the love of money is a root of all kinds of evil" (1 Timothy 6:10). How then can we have peace when our possessions are threatened? What hope do we have that enables us to retain our joy despite the prospect of financial and material loss? Martin Luther's response demonstrated that he knew the truths of Psalm 49.

Luther's focus was on eternity—how his actions in the present would be viewed by King Jesus at the great day of judgment. He didn't live under the pressure of the moment. Because of his confidence in a sovereignly gracious God, he feared no man. And because the promises of God's Word assured him that God would supply all his needs according to his riches in Jesus, he had no concern about his needs for food, clothing, or shelter. Because God is the gracious King of all the earth, we can respond to threats to our material possessions by following God's Word without fear and with a focus on eternity.

Follow God's Word (vv. 1–4)

The psalmist grabs our attention when he insists that what he has to say is of the utmost importance to every human being, "low and high, rich and poor" (v. 2). What is so important is our response to material possessions, both our use of them and especially their use against us as God's people. It is of great importance because he knows the power material things have to tempt us either to lust or fear. They are powerful because we are material people in a material world. If God is King over all the earth, then he is King over all *we* have, and King over all *who* have.

The words translated "wisdom" and "understanding" are plural in Hebrew, which heightens importance. This is "weighty wisdom."[2] For instance, *Elohim* is the plural name of God. It is akin to the royal "we." He is saying that the statements he will make about material wealth will not be opinions but infallible directives; they are divine. Some may say the author is being pompous, but notice how he can make such a bold claim. It is only because he has "turn[ed] his ear to a proverb" (v. 4, NIV). God has given him these words. The preacher has first been instructed. Likewise, we are urged to sit under God's teaching, not the teaching of a mere human.

Fear No Person (vv. 5–12)

Here, the people of God are under threat by wicked people who have substantial resources. Since this psalm is authored by the sons of Korah, who ministered in Israel during the era of Assyrian oppression (late eighth century BC), the psalmists could be referring particularly to the Assyrian threat under Sennacherib. That would be fitting, since Jerusalem was surrounded and the Assyrians "trust[ed] in their wealth" and "boast[ed] in their great riches" (v. 6, NIV). Sennacherib mocked the Judahites' reliance upon God, saying that "no god of any nation or kingdom [had] been able to deliver his people" from Assyria's hand (2 Chronicles 32:15).[3] We can be similarly tempted to not trust in God in three areas: witnessing, bitterness, and moral compromise.

Christians can be tempted to mute their witness under the intimidation of wealthier or more powerful people. For instance, those in leadership roles are invited to high-level gatherings and are listened to and honored. It may be an acceptance speech for an award, an editorial in the newspaper, or an interview on the radio. Christians, when given such opportunities, can be tempted to not give any hint that they belong to Christ, for fear that they might not get invited back. Chuck Colson once confronted a friend who was a pastor on this topic. The minister was close to a sitting US president who had just signed legislation that seemed to Colson like a moral compromise. Colson asked his friend why he had not questioned the president. To Colson's astonishment, the minister answered, "I'm having dinner with the president next month."[4] He thought that he was advancing the kingdom incrementally by hiding his light under a bushel (Matthew 5:15).

Another way we can buckle under the ostensible power of material things is to become bitter. We may think, "I can't witness to those people. They will just look down on me." We can also withdraw from our surrounding cultures by thinking that the wealth behind evil systems makes the cause of justice impossible.

Finally, we may compromise because we fear losing money through a lawsuit, being written out of a will, or losing customers. I have a friend who acquired a sizable business and informed his new employees that his corporate culture would not include certain outwardly immoral practices. When someone asked how he could say such things and not get sued, he said, "When the Lord saved me in high school, I was so thrilled that I promised that if he ever gave me a place of influence I would not compromise my faith. I would make him known there. I am not afraid of lawsuits. I dread my Savior saying, 'I am ashamed of you.'"

Why should we as God's people be intimidated by wealth or influence when those things are ultimately powerless? True power is the ability to conquer and overturn death. Money and political might cannot. No matter how much a wealthy man loves his terminally ill son, "No one can redeem the life of another or give to God a ransom for them" (v. 7, NIV). No matter how many safeguards he attempts to put on his money, he will "[leave his] wealth to others" when he dies (v. 10, NIV). No matter how elaborate their tombs or how many lands and buildings are named in their memory, the wicked wealthy man will not live on (v. 11). Death will overcome him and erase his memory: "People, despite their wealth, do not endure; they are like the beasts that perish" (v. 12, NIV).

However, if you belong to Jesus, you have been ransomed and your life is now hidden with Christ in God (Colossians 3:3). No evil person can erase your life. You will live on with Christ. History proves that your life in Christ becomes even more powerful if you are martyred. God is able to establish the work of our hands in such a way that it becomes eternally significant even after we die and the world is no more (Psalm 90:17).

We can then say with the psalmist, "What can mere man do to me?" (Psalm 56:4, NASB) We can boldly share our faith despite intimidation. We can confidently acknowledge that God owns the cattle on a thousand hills and that his resources outnumber all those who stand against us (Psalm 50:10). And we must never compromise morally, knowing that even if we die for what is right, we will live on, and the cause of righteousness will, too (Revelation 14:13).

Focus on Eternity (vv. 13–20)

Finally, the psalmist encourages us to be bold in the face of intimidators by contrasting our eternal state with theirs. The first contrast is between our respective shepherds. Death will shepherd the unrighteous to the grave; the significance of their lives will be no more. They will live on in the death they had in life by suffering hell. On the other hand, the Good Shepherd will "redeem [us] from the realm of the dead" (v. 15, NIV). Our future existence will not be boring or insignificant. There will be work for us to do, including ruling with Christ (1 Corinthians 6:2).

Next, he challenges us to contrast the praise we will receive in glory with the praise the ungodly receive now. The lives of the wicked can be enjoyable while they last. Their accomplishments and accouterments may be rewarded by people's praise, but that ends at death. On the other hand, Christ promises to praise us after death for works done through the grace of God to the glory of God. The idea that God will praise us some day is beautiful and humbling (John 12:43; Romans 2:29; 9:21; 1 Peter 1:7).

Many years ago, psychiatrist John White said three important things about the use of material resources. First, the way we use our resources reveals the reality and significance of our faith: "Our goal in life will determine our view of life" and "enslavement to the visible makes faith in the invisible suspect."[5] The Bible never condemns wealth in and of itself. It condemns the wrong use of it, either in abusing others (Amos 2:6–7) or in failing to use it to further the things that burden God. John Wesley preached, "Having, first, gained all you can, and, secondly saved all you can, then give all you can."[6] Handling abundance in a way that will be eternally praised requires dependence on the grace of the Holy Spirit.

Second, White also observed that Christians are rarely happy as materialists. They may live like this world is all there is, but their hearts tell them that they are called to another country:

> The misery of a Christian torn between heaven and material things can be pitiful. A self-made Cantonese importer invited my wife and me to dinner once. His house was breathtaking–a fortress outside and all softness and luxury within. In the foyer stood an artificial tree, perhaps five feet high, whose leaves and flowers were exquisitely fashioned from clusters of semiprecious stones. Ornate cabinets displayed valuable treasures. His tableware looked like solid gold, but we did not dare to ask. Our host was about sixty years old and displayed a considerable knowledge of Scripture, yet as he talked there was no glow of joy about him. He told us he planned to make enough money to spend his closing years in serving the Lord "without being a burden on anybody." . . . He never did get to serve the Lord. He had sold his heritage for stone and metal trinkets inside a painted fortress. He would have agreed that spiritual things matter more than material security, but his behavior contradicted his professed beliefs. Riches had coiled like a living vine around his heart, slowly strangling his love for God and people.[7]

Third, White said, "There is no virtue in poverty unless in the course of our obedience to God we have to endure poverty because of a greater end."[8] Jesus became poor not because it was virtuous to do so; he became poor in order to save us. If you are called to serve God in some particular way, go for it! If you fail to make as much money as you could or if you lose something material along the way, remember that you will get it back and more in heaven.

You may be familiar with the ancient fable of King Midas. In spite of his great wealth, when asked by a stranger for a wish, Midas asked for a golden touch. He wanted everything that he touched to turn to gold. At first it pleased him. Blocks of wood became ingots of gold bullion. Rocks became like freshly mined gold. The straw in a manger became gold thread—all with a simple touch. But eventually his touch became a curse. The king grew hungry, and spying a delectably ripe peach he reached for it, only to have it morph into a golden ball. Thirsty, he cupped his hands to draw water from a fresh spring, but the water turned to solid gold. Returning home, he came upon his daughter who was crying bitter tears because the delicate roses she cherished in her garden had all been turned to gold by her greedy father. King Midas's heart broke for his child, so he reached his arm around her to comfort her, but his golden touch became the ultimate curse as his very own daughter ceased to live and was reduced to solid gold. In desperation, the king cried out to the stranger to release him of the curse of the golden touch. The stranger told Midas that if he would plunge himself into the river all would return to its original state. The king threw himself into the river as if being baptized with the baptism of repentance and all was restored, even his beloved child.[9]

Have we become so intimidated or intoxicated with the world's gold that we are in danger of destroying the beauty that surrounds us and robbing ourselves and even our children of true life, both here and in eternity? Christ calls us to repent and plunge ourselves into the waters of God's grace, that he might show us what it means to be truly wealthy in his kingdom. God's word applied to our hearts by the Holy Spirit produces the "wisdom" and "understanding" of this psalm to see life as transitory (v. 3; cf. Colossians 1:9). Because all of us naturally lack spiritual wisdom and understanding, Paul teaches us to pray for it from the Father. If he is a Father who is generous enough to bring us "into the kingdom of the Son he loves" (Colossians 1:13, NIV), he will surely delight to give us the attitude we need to live in it with joy.

Questions for Reflection/Discussion

1. Can you think of ways that material possessions, or lack thereof, have caused you distress?

2. What is the eternal perspective provided for us in this psalm?

3. In what way does Jesus prove that he will withhold no good thing from those who walk upright (Psalm 84:11)?

Prayer

What material need(s) do you have or are you fearful of? Pray through the stanzas of this psalm, remembering not to put your trust in wealth (v. 6), but trusting God to supply your needs (Philippians 4:19). Ask God to give you peace in the knowledge of who he is, and what he has done for you and will continue to do for you, and for an eternal perspective about your present reality.

14

Pardon for Sin and a Peace That Endures

Psalm 51

Restore to me the joy of your salvation,
and grant me a willing spirit, to sustain me.
(Psalm 51:12, NIV)

PSALM 49 SHOWED us a Savior who delights to give us everything we need in this life and the life to come. Psalm 51 shows us that part of that provision includes repentance.

We often find ourselves resistant to repentance, wondering why we need it. Some years ago, the deacons in the church I pastored were asked to investigate the needs of an elderly widow. They went to her home and found her living conditions deplorable and her health in a desperate state. Her house was dark and dank and its smell was putrid. We were deeply concerned for her but also deeply confused. Why had she never asked for help? We came to find out that she had never asked for help because she was embarrassed about her condition. It was simply too painful for her to open the door and let anyone in to see her state.

It is a picture of what we often do with our sin. We somehow think that God will be deluded into thinking more highly of us if we keep certain doors of our hearts closed to him. We may be too embarrassed, afraid, or proud to confess our sins to him. The reality is, he already knows the sins of our hearts. To refuse to confess them, then, is to distance ourselves from God and miss out on the blessings of repentance.

When this woman finally accepted help, her whole countenance changed. She was delivered from the hopeless state she was living in and experienced joy for the first time in a long time. This is the great paradox of repentance: when we hide our sin, we live in misery, but when we bring it to God and find forgiveness and renewal, we are restored to "the joy of [our] salvation" (Psalm 51:10).

Psalm 51 teaches us how to repent. Let me remind you of the tragic events in David's life which occasioned his writing of this psalm. One spring evening when David should have been leading his armies in war, he strolled out on his balcony and noticed a beautiful woman bathing. He sent messengers to bring her to him. He slept with her and she conceived a child. To cover up his sin, he sent for her husband, Uriah the Hittite, who was in the battle. His scheme was for Uriah to sleep with his wife so that it would appear the child was legitimately conceived. However, Uriah was a loyal soldier. He would not indulge in pleasures while his comrades were at war so he slept with the servants rather than in his own house. When that scheme failed, David instructed his commander to put Uriah at the front of the battle line where the engagement was fiercest, then withdraw so that Uriah would be killed. It worked; Uriah was killed in battle. David was free to take Bathsheba as his wife and make it appear that the child was legitimately theirs (2 Samuel 11).

The only problem was that while no one else knew the truth, God did. And he revealed it to his prophet Nathan. Nathan confronted David with a parable about two men in the same town. One was rich and had many sheep and cattle. The other was poor and had only one ewe lamb. It was like a member of the family. It grew up with the children, ate from their table, and even slept in the poor man's arms at night. One day, the rich man was visited by a friend from out of town. Not wanting to use one of his own sheep, he stole the poor man's lamb and slaughtered it.

David loved sheep, and taking the parable to be an actual account he flew into a rage and judged that that man should pay four times over. Nathan then delivered God's message: "You are the man!" (2 Samuel 12:7). Nathan told David that he had despised the word of the Lord and had therefore despised the Lord himself. In the account of 2 Samuel 12:13, we only have this brief confession, "I have sinned against the LORD." Psalm 51 is his full confession. In it we find a record of what repentance is—a confession of wrong and a restoration of fellowship with the Lord.

Appeal to God's Mercy (vv. 1–2)

Three different words for "sin" are used in verses 1–2 covering the full orbit of our disobedience to God's will. These are not different degrees of sin. These words characterize the various ways that our sins offend.

Transgression (peshah)

The first word that appears in verse 1 is "transgressions." This word refers to our relationship with God and describes a departure from his revealed will, even direct rebellion against it. This sin sounds like this on our lips or in our hearts, "I know what God says, *but. . . .*" It is direct rebellion. David knew God forbade adultery. He knew God's prohibitions against adultery and murder, but he did them anyway. And we do the same. Our consciences convict us of slander, thievery, jealousy, and wayward affections. But we choose to engage in them anyway.

Iniquity (hawon)

The second word occurs in verse 2, and is translated "iniquity." It describes our relationship to ourselves—that is, that our hearts are crooked in their motives and wicked in their deepest intents. David tried to cover his guilt with his conniving words, the very thing he accused his enemies of in Psalm 5:9 (NIV): "Not a word from their mouth can be trusted; their heart is filled with malice. Their throat is an open grave; with their tongues they tell lies." Our hearts are just as crooked to devise evil schemes that will tarnish another's reputation or justify an affair.

Sin

The third word in verse 2 describes our relation to the law. Literally, it comes from the world of archery and means "to miss the mark." It describes our failure to keep any commandment fully. David missed the mark of the law. The sin of adultery is not just taking another man's wife; it is the failure to treasure her as his wife. You have not succeeded at keeping that commandment until you treasure every woman as a human made in the image of God and as someone else's wife, daughter, sister, or mother.

David lived in a time when Israel followed Mosaic Law. Under the Law, certain sacrifices were prescribed for particular sins. However, in David's case, there were no sacrifices prescribed for adultery and murder. Only death was prescribed. There was no hope for David in the Law. There were not enough lambs in Israel to atone for David's crimes. David needed God himself to become a lamb and stand between David and his sin.

That is precisely what he begs in verse 1. It is evident in the words David writes, as well as the order in which he writes them. *David* is at the beginning of verse 1: "Have mercy on *me*." At the end of verse 1 and in all of verse 2 is *David's sin*, described in the terms we just mentioned. Between David and his sin is *God* in his "unfailing love" and his "compassion" (v. 1, NIV). This is God's mercy, putting himself between us and our sins. It is the same order of the publican's prayer in Luke 18:13 (NIV): "God, have mercy on me, a sinner."

When you have sinned, there is only one thing to do. There is no sacrifice you can bring, no penance you can perform, no scheme to cover it up. However, you have the ability to appeal to God's mercy, asking him to put his Son between you and your sin.

Confess Your Sin (vv. 3–6)

Verse 3 (NIV) explains David's urgent plea for mercy: "For I know my transgressions, and my sin is always before me." David recognizes his sin and confesses it as his own. He does so at three levels.

I Am Aware (v. 3)

The first is so obvious that it might seem trite: namely, that you must be aware of your sin. But this is precisely where the battle begins. Notice that David uses the right pronouns here (emphasis added): "*my* iniquity," "*my* sin," "*my* transgressions." Acknowledging sin is not pleasant. In fact, it can be crushing. It often takes others to make us aware of them, just as Nathan had to confront David about his sin.

I Sinned against You (v. 4)

The second component of a true confession is to acknowledge that you have sinned directly against God. Some are offended by this because they take it that David did not recognize his offense against Bathsheba and Uriah. The first thing that must be said in response is that God himself labeled it a personal offense. Remember, Nathan reported God's words, "you despised *me* and took the wife of Uriah the Hittite to be your own" (2 Samuel 12:10, NIV, emphasis added). The second fact is that every sin against a person is a sin against an image-bearer of God. James makes it clear that when we offend others with our tongues, we curse those made in the image of God (James 3:9).

I Alone Am to Blame (v. 5)

Further, we must admit that we alone are responsible for our sin. In verse 5 (NIV) David articulates the doctrine of original sin: "Surely I was sinful at birth, sinful from the time my mother conceived me." This doctrine is explained elsewhere in the Old Testament as well (Genesis 8:21; Job 14:4; 15:14; 25:4). David in no way implies that the act of conception is a sinful activity. Nor does he attempt to explain the manner in which the sinful nature is transferred from parent to child. He simply states the fact that we can all observe: no one teaches their children to sin; they come "pre-programmed" to do it.

Therefore, David's lust could not be blamed on weariness or bad friends—he was responsible. No one had to teach him how to prepare a murderous scheme. The whole evil play from adultery to murder was written by the pen of his own sinful heart. If your confession is true, it will not be characterized by excuses. No mitigating circumstances will be named. You must simply confess that whatever sin you committed arose from wanting to go your way, not God's way.

Pray for a New Record (vv. 7–9)

We can ask God to come in between his wrath and our sin and we must confess that sin is all that God says it is. But we need more. To be restored in our relationship with God we need our sinful record changed. David uses three images that communicate the thoroughness of God's forgiveness. These three images perfectly address all the categories of transgression, iniquity, and sin we distinguished earlier.

Cleansing

David first prays, "cleanse me with hyssop" (v. 7, NIV). Hyssop is a sort of vine that grows on walls in Israel. Its absorbency made it useful for sprinkling blood and water as it was prescribed in certain cleansing rites in the Old Testament. However, because of the word he uses, I think David wants us to think of more than Mosaic cleansing. It is a word similar to the generic word translated "sin" (*chattah*). David is literally praying, "Purge me, de-sin me." He is asking God to solve his inward problem with sin, the crooked nature of his heart.

This is a great example for us to follow in our prayer. We need more than mere forgiveness for the particular sin we have committed. We need our sin problem cured! So we affirm with Paul that there is a law at work in us, making us prisoners of the law of sin and causing us to cry out, "What a wretched man I am! Who will rescue me from this body that is subject to death?" (Romans 7:24, NIV).

Washing

Next, David prays, "wash me" (v. 7). Not only are we contaminated on the inside; we are contaminated on the outside. We have yielded up our eyes, ears, mouths, and minds to breaking the law. David prays for all the washings that are prescribed in the law to purify a sinner from outward sin to be applied to him by God himself. This too is a helpful way to pray. We need God to cure our indwelling sin and to wash us of all of those sinful activities we have engaged in and corrupted ourselves with.

Blotting

Finally, David uses an image that comes from the days when manuscripts were produced on papyri: "blot out all my iniquity" (v. 9). If a mistake was made, it could be rubbed out, or erased. David's record was stained by his sin. He could never be admitted into heaven with it. David asked for something that was contrary to God's character. God cannot simply blot out sin and forget about it. It has to be atoned for. David was praying for something only God could provide. It would require that God himself, in all his holiness, substitute his record for ours. David was praying for what Christ, the perfect Lamb of God, would someday supply.

Jesus Christ, God made flesh, our Immanuel, is the answer to all of these requests. The answer to our inward sickness is found after Paul's "wretched man" plea: "Thanks be to God, who delivers me through Jesus Christ our Lord! . . . [B]ecause through Christ Jesus the law of the Spirit who gives life has set you free from the law of sin and death" (Romans 7:25; 8:2, NIV). Christ is the answer to our need for cleansing, because "the blood of Jesus, his Son, purifies us from all sin" (1 John 1:7, NIV). And Christ is our hope for a clean record:

> But now apart from the law the righteousness of God has been made known. . . . This righteousness is given through faith in Jesus Christ to all who believe. . . . God presented Christ as a sacrifice of atonement, through the shedding of his blood—to be received by faith. He did this to demonstrate his righteousness, because in his forbearance he had left the sins committed beforehand unpunished. (Romans 3:21–22; 25, NIV)

Pray for Renewal (vv. 10–11)

After a time of rebellion, we must pray for renewal of our Christian life. It seems counterintuitive to ask God for joy when we have been rebelling, but we must think of it in these terms: "God, restore me to the joy of my salvation so that I will be so satisfied in you I won't be tempted to rebel again, because I will be convinced that there is nothing better in this life than being filled with the joy only you can give." In verse 8, David asks God to "let [him] hear joy and gladness." That prayer is the fountainhead of many requests between verses 7–12. He prays for many things because he has lost so much.

Ask for a Miracle (v. 10)

We noted earlier that we must ask God to cure the sin in us which we are born into. That is what we are encouraged to ask again in verse 10—"Create in me a pure heart, O God"—only here the request is bolder. The word translated "create" is the same as that used in Genesis 1:1 (*bara*). David asks for nothing less than a miracle. He asks God to create a new heart out of nothing. Do we dare to pray that way? Yes! God promises he can and will do it, saying through Ezekiel, "I will give you a new heart and put a new spirit in you" (Ezekiel 36:26, NIV). Paul tells us that there is nothing good about the old heart. It is infinitely irredeemable: "I know that nothing good dwells in me, that is, in my flesh. For I have the desire to do what is right, but not the ability to carry it out" (Romans 7:18). Paul teaches us that God must continually give us a new heart. Our hearts have a pathological tendency to harden toward God.

Ask for a New Relationship (v. 11)

In verse 11 (NIV), David asks, "Do not cast me from your presence or take your Holy Spirit from me." There are two possible errors in interpreting this verse. One is to think that David is only concerned about his kingly office—that he doesn't want to lose it as Saul did when God withdrew the Spirit from him. But this psalm is entirely personal. There is no hint that David is merely concerned for his office.

The second error is to think that David is afraid of losing his salvation. However, the Bible does not teach that God gives and removes his Spirit randomly. In Romans 8:9–11 Paul states definitively that if you are a Christian, you have the Spirit, the same Spirit that raised Jesus from the dead. In view of that passage, if the Spirit were removed, it would be a failure on God's part, not the sinner's.

So what is David asking? It seems to me that David has become acutely aware of how prone he is to make destructive choices. He has also come to realize that God's presence in his life, specifically through the Holy Spirit, is the only thing that can empower him to live a holy life. This is one positive purpose of God's allowing us to fall into temptation. It teaches us that we have no power against sin in ourselves and causes us to place greater trust in God.[1]

There may be something else here as well. The *Westminster Confession of Faith* says that in our sin we experience God's "Fatherly displeasure."[2] A student once asked me how it could be true that we cannot earn more favor with God and yet at times experience his displeasure. My answer was that it is just like the relationship with a good father. He may be displeased with a child at times for rebellious or self-destructive behavior, but it does not change his love. In fact, it is the steadfastness of his love that makes his displeasure the more acute. David is praying, then, for his relationship with the Father to be restored.

Teach Others (vv. 12–17)

Our renewal is not a secret we are to keep to ourselves. The only sense in which we are debtors to grace is that we owe it to God to tell others about it.

Granted Repentance (v. 12)

Sometimes we torment ourselves wondering if we have repented adequately. In this verse David recognizes accurately that repentance is a gift, asking God to "grant [him] a willing spirit, to sustain [him]" (v. 12, NIV; cf. Acts 5:31; 2 Timothy 3:25). The dynamics of this verse are seen most clearly in the life of Peter. Christ's sovereignty over his repentance and restoration is revealed in Luke 22:32, when Christ prophesies that Peter will turn back because he prayed for him. Peter's restoration is recognized by the apostles in Luke 24:34: he "appeared to Simon." John 21:15–19 gives us a detailed description of the way Jesus restored Peter. We are taught, then, to pray for Christ to grant us repentance unto life, not to try and muster it up on our own.

Wooed Sinners (v. 13)

Verse 13 also has close connections with Peter. David proclaims that once God has restored him to the joy of his salvation and granted him "a willing spirit," then David "will teach transgressors [God's] ways." This is also seen in the Lord's command to Peter: "And when you have turned again, strengthen your brothers" (Luke 22:32). God takes us through our temptation, repentance, and restoration so that we might show others the way. The redemptive purpose of your restoration is to show others where to find it.

Declared Praise (vv. 14–17)

Like David, telling the story of God's grace with power starts with "a broken and contrite heart" (v. 17). When you recognize the waywardness, guilt, and destructive tendency of your heart alongside God's steadfast love and forgiveness to cleanse you, you can say with David, "Open my lips, Lord, and my mouth will declare your praise" (v. 15, NIV).

Pray for Those Affected (vv. 18–19)

Finally, our sin always affects someone else. Whether our sin is inward or outward, it always affects others negatively. David now sees this and prays, "May it please you to prosper Zion," David writes, "to build up the walls of Jerusalem" (v. 18, NIV). As a king, David's sin affected many people.

It is easy enough to see how murder or theft or caustic speech can harm others, but what about inward sin? Can it stay inward? No, we are always going in one direction or another. Inward sin, if unrepented for, will one day be impossible to keep hidden. If you are prayerless, your family and friends will suffer. If you are engaged in secret fantasies, your marriage or future marriage will suffer. If you are bitter, your relationships and perhaps even your health will suffer, which will affect everyone you meet. If you are given to cynicism, your children will pick up on it and imitate it.

For God to Be Praised (v. 19)

When you fail and others are affected, pray that God would heal. He alone is able to build up the broken walls of his people.

When he does so, the bond becomes stronger than the original. Pray not just that the effects of your sin would be mitigated, but that God's people would be repaired so that God's worship would not be hindered.

I think this is the way David envisioned it working: The confession of his sin would provoke Israel to flee to the altars and confess their sins. His sin would remind them that they had committed the same categories of sin. While they may not have shed someone's blood, they had tarnished reputations and hated their brothers. While they may not have slept in anyone else's bed, they had lusted in their hearts or committed adultery with unfaithful worship. Likewise, when our fellow Christians sin, even if it affects us in a negative way, it must not move us to judgment but to more vigorous repentance of our own sins.

At the first church I pastored, I found the pulpit hidden away in a storeroom. I pulled it out, and our sexton painstakingly restored it. It had hand-carved Christian symbolism all over it, from wheat and grapes symbolizing communion, to the passion plant representing the wounds of Christ, to the lily reminding of his resurrection, to the dragons under the reading table representing the power of the Word of God.

There was one symbol, however, that I did not recognize at first. I eventually discovered that it was a pelican, one of the oldest symbols of the atonement in the church. If you looked carefully, you could see that the pelican was plucking out her breast. It was once thought that in times of famine, pelicans would do this to feed their young with their own blood. It is the symbol of Christ. Christ gave his own life's blood to cleanse us from our inward pollution, to wash us from our outward offenses against the law and blot out our records so that we could live in eternal fellowship with him. Appeal to that mercy, confess your sin, pray for a new record, and experience new life in Jesus Christ.

Questions for Reflection/Discussion

1. Do you ever feel similarly to the woman at the beginning of this chapter, with regard to confessing your sin to God?

2. To what does David appeal to be forgiven of his sin? Why do you think David makes this appeal *before* confessing his sin in detail?

3. How does this psalm show us we can have peace when we ask for a new record?

4. How does this psalm give us hope when we ask for renewal?

Prayer

This psalm is an extremely important prayer for every Christian to learn, because it teaches us how to repent—something we will do our entire Christian lives. Follow the structure of David's prayer to confess to God any area of sin that you have not yet acknowledged and turned from. As you do:

- Ask for the Lord's mercy (vv. 1–2).
- Confess your sin (vv. 3–6).
- Thank God for the new record you can have in Jesus (vv. 7–9; see also 1 John 1:7, 9).
- Pray for renewal (vv. 10–11).
- Pray for opportunities to teach others about God's grace and forgiveness (vv. 12–17).

15

The Light of Life

Psalm 56

When I am afraid, I put my trust in you.
(Psalm 56:3)

ARTHUR MATTHEWS WOULD have found a soul mate in David through Psalm 56. He and his family were the last missionaries with China Inland Mission to leave when the communists took over at the end of the Second World War. Under Mao Zedong's oppressive regime, the Matthews suffered intensely. Cut off from friends and support, they barely survived in their one-room hovel with their little girl Lilah. A stool was their only piece of furniture, and heat came from a tiny stove fueled by dung Arthur scavenged from the streets. Despite their deprivations, the Matthews discovered a deeper truth: the Spirit sustained their souls with his Word.

Seeing their story as a literal fulfillment of the promise made in Jeremiah 17:8, Isobel Kuhn, another missionary, wrote a book about the Matthews "not simply to tell another story of the trials that Christians and missionaries faced under communism in China. Its true purpose is to describe God's provision for His children that allows them to 'put forth green leaves when all others around are dried up and dying from the drought.'"[1] Her book and David's psalm remind us that in the dark nights of the soul, God is ready to sustain us, not merely with enough grace to survive but enough to thrive. If you feel alone, afraid, or desperate, you will find sympathy from David in Psalm 56. In this psalm, David demonstrates that the Savior of Psalm 51 who loves you enough to forgive you at the ultimate cost to himself is surely worthy of our trust in times of fear, loneliness, and desperation.

David wrote this psalm in reflection on his captivity in Gath (1 Samuel 21:1–15). David found food and refuge with Ahimelech, a priest in Nob, while he was running for his life from Saul. Refreshed, he then fled to Gath, the capital of Philistia. As soon as he arrived there, the servants of King Achish remembered the song Israel sang about David, "Saul has slain his thousands, and David his ten thousands" (1 Samuel 18:7, NASB). The "ten thousands" included his killing of Goliath of Gath, the Philistines' mightiest man. To say the least, David was not a hero in Gath. Neither did it help that he was gesturing with Goliath's sword, which Ahimelech had given him for protection. In the end, David had to pretend he was insane to be released alive.

Bible scholars are universally perplexed about David's going to Gath. I think the best explanation is Derek Kidner's: it "took the courage of despair."[2] David was alone, afraid, and desperate. We know he was alone because Ahimelech notes it as an oddity (1 Samuel 21:2). David never traveled on approved missions for Saul without an army. This time he had fled in secrecy and no one was with him. He had no companion, no army, no fellow countrymen. He was all alone . . . and afraid. We know that from the central verse of this psalm: "When I am afraid, I will trust in you" (v. 3, NIV1984). It is this solitude and fear that now make David desperate. Can you identify?

After David fled Gath, he went to the cave at Adullam. Maybe he wrote Psalm 56 there. Perhaps it was so dark he could barely see his hand in front of his face, and a single ray of light pierced his darkness like a needle. This light would have reminded him that the light of God's word—which is not only written in Scripture but incarnated in Christ (John 1:1–5)—can pierce the otherwise impenetrable darkness of the soul, causing David to conclude this psalm by saying, "For you have delivered me from death and my feet from stumbling, that I may walk before God in the light of life" (v. 13, NIV).

This psalm is organized by a chorus, which appears in verses 3–4 (NIV; see also vv. 10–11):

> When I am afraid, I put my trust in you.
>   In God, whose word I praise—
> in God I trust and am not afraid.
>   What can mere mortals do to me?

In this chorus, David makes a bold declaration: he is not afraid of mortal man because he trusts in God and his Word. At this point in history, David did not have much of God's written Word. However, it was enough to reveal God's character and enough light to sustain his faith. You and I have much more reason to be courageous and not fear man's schemes. We have the complete revelation of God, who became incarnate in Jesus Christ.

When Afraid (vv. 1–4)

In the midst of his fear, David asks, "What can mortal man do to me?" (v. 3, NIV). On one level, the answer to his question would seem to be, "Well, a lot!" We have seen humans do horrendous things. Perhaps you have been the victim of their evil. Despots murder millions of innocents. White-robed thugs lynch and oppress in a diabolical lust for racial supremacy. Terrorists take down airplanes, killing hundreds. A serial killer viciously murders scores of women over decades. Humans do a lot to humans, so there is a lot to be afraid of.

But there is nothing that man can do to us *ultimately*. If Christ is your Savior, nothing else—whether physical harm, emotional abuse, or even death—has the final say for you. David had a concept of heaven; he was able to look beyond this life to that which is to come. However, notice that David says God offers something in this life as well, something stronger than life's tragedies—God's "word" (vv. 4, 10).

God's word—what God says to us—assures us of God's ultimate, merciful protection. In verse 1, David's realization of his vulnerability thrusts him on God's mercy. Many years later, Peter will assure us that God's eternal mercy is a secure refuge:

Praise be to the God and Father of our Lord Jesus Christ! In his great mercy, he has given us new birth into a living hope through the resurrection of Jesus Christ from the dead, and into an inheritance that can never perish, spoil or fade–kept in heaven for you, who through faith are shielded by God's power until the coming of the salvation that is ready to be revealed in the last time. In this you greatly rejoice, though now for a little while you may have had to suffer grief in all kinds of trials. (1 Peter 1:3–6, NIV)

Even if someone takes your life, this is not the end. To die is to pass immediately into glory, and someday you will receive a resurrected body (2 Corinthians 5:8). No mortal can prevent that. You are physically protected into all of eternity by the mercy of God. That is true hope.

God's Word points us to God's mercy, and it also points us to the peace God provides. This peace is an emotional refuge more profound than any circumstance. In verse 2 (NIV), David seems to say that the slander he is experiencing from Saul and his men is worse than the fear of physical capture: "My adversaries pursue me all day long; in their pride many are attacking me." Sometimes, words *do* hurt us more than sticks or stones! However, when a believer fixes his or her mind on the character of God, no matter what trials, attacks, spiritual battles, or illnesses may harass us, God promises he will give us peace (Isaiah 26:3). Sometimes it is called a peace that passes understanding (Philippians 4:7). It is the image of the eye of a storm. The child of God may be surrounded by trouble, but he is at peace. "You prepare a table before me in the presence of my enemies" (Psalm 23:5). God's mercy is what creates the eye of the storm and makes space for that peace. The Christian always has a safe place from which to join David on the chorus, "When I am afraid . . . *I put my trust in you.*" (v. 3, NIV, emphasis added).

When Alone (vv. 5–11)

The Bible also provides assurance of God's presence when we are alone. At times, we can be as alone in our tears as David is: "Record my misery; list my tears on your scroll—are they not in your record?" (v. 8, NIV). In the average Christian's lifetime, there will be many secret tears, but no tears are more bitter than those shed with no one near who understands and no one available to sympathize. Even in the midst of this, we find one of the most precious promises of all Scripture—as the ESV puts it, "put my tears in your bottle" (v. 8). God takes account of every teardrop and stores them in his fatherly memory. Actually, the original language contains a bigger promise: "Put my tears in your *wineskin.*" A wineskin expands over time. I don't know about you, but my secret tears could not be contained in a small bottle. The promise is that God's heart continually expands to provide storage for our tears. How beautiful that God should tell us that. Because this is true, we can sing with David, "Man cannot trample my heart because God stores up all my tears!"

The very next verse describes a strength that comes from weakness vocalized to God through tears: while God records his lament, David rejoices that "my enemies will turn back in the day when I call" (v. 9). I was once in a business meeting where a staff member was making a plea to a superior. Despite the reasonableness of his presentation, he made little headway. Noticing the boss's disinterest, others who were opposed to the man's suggestion felt strengthened in their position, banded together, and confidently spoke up against him.

Eventually, assuming defeat, he sat down with tears in his eyes. Up to that point, no argument had turned the boss's head. But the tears did immediately. In an instant, the inattentive superior became an advocate. Flummoxed, the opponents desperately began to backpedal, looking for safe retreat positions. The difference here is that we don't have to turn God from opposition or indifference to advocacy. The text tells us he is *already* for us. Realizing God is for you is reason to turn to him in your loneliness; it will turn your enemies to flight.

When Desperate (vv. 12–13)

David's final reason for courageous trust is that God always delivers his people. What makes David's thanksgiving for rescue so remarkable is that he expresses it *before* deliverance comes. David had hope! We often act as if "thank you" is a perfunctory expression, but David shows us what a state of genuine gratitude looks like. It is always worth remembering that we will never be anything other than a delivered people. When we are living with that constant consciousness, we can resist the perennial temptation to mistrust God's Word. Taking time to remember our past escapes will bolster us in the midst of trial. Remember how God's Word has saved you before when all looked impossible. He will do it again. No situation can disable the word's ability, by the power of the Holy Spirit, to deliver from fear and loneliness.

There is a story of nine mutineers who turned against Captain Bligh in the famous mutiny on his ship, the *Bounty*. After commandeering the ship, the mutineers found their way to Pitcairn Island, a speck in the Pacific Ocean just two miles wide and one mile long. After several years of drinking and brawling, only one of the nine was left alive, John Adams. Twelve men and twenty-three women made up the indigenous population of the island.

One day, while digging through one of the trunks from the ship, Adams found the *Bounty*'s Bible. He read it and was converted. He was so thrilled to be freed from his dark life that he began teaching it to the children of Pitcairn. All of the children, along with their parents, were eventually converted.[3] Today, with a population of about a hundred, virtually everyone on this tiny island in the middle of the Pacific Ocean is a Christian. The word of God delivers from fear and loneliness and leads to the light of life.

In the final verse of the psalm, we see the result of being delivered from our fear, loneliness, and desperation—we are set back on our feet to serve God. God not only liberated David from the Philistines; he rescued him from despair. Surely there were many times in David's life when it would have seemed easier to die, or at least to stop serving God, than to go on living. Perhaps you have felt the same. When we are overcome with feelings of fear, loneliness, and desperation, our focus is turned inward.

However, God's Word became David's lifeline. Not only does God's Word lead away from hopelessness; it leads into a purposeful light: "For you have delivered me from death and my feet from stumbling, that I may walk before God in the light of life" (v. 13, NIV). It is in the Bible that we find Christ the Word become flesh. In him, we find everything we need for a life of trust. The Word of God revealing Christ can break through and provide light to the darkest of life situations.

Questions for Reflection/Discussion

1. What promise does this psalm and other passages such as Psalm 23:5, Isaiah 26:3, and Philippians 4:7 give us regarding peace when we are afraid?

2. How have you seen in this psalm, and in others we have already studied, that Jesus is near to us when we are alone?

3. What is the hope we have when we turn to Christ in times of fear, loneliness, and desperation?

Prayer

Use the chorus of this psalm (vv. 3–4; 10–11) as the guide for your own prayer. Declare your trust in God in the middle of your fears, and ask him to give you peace through his presence and the light of his Word. Praise him for his nearness and that he sees each of your tears (v. 8). Consider also who else needs to hear this message, and find a time to share your hope with that person.

16

Surviving
a Surprise Attack

Psalm 64

Let the righteous one rejoice in the LORD
and take refuge in him!
(Psalm 64:10)

IN PSALM 64, David warns us to be ready for an attack from any direction. One of my church members once told me he wondered if any of these psalms on enemies would ever apply to him. He lived a relatively quiet life, but he met an enemy while selling his house. He was preparing to move to another part of the country and put his house up for sale. A man who had made a small fortune by intimidating and threatening business tactics made him an offer with specific contingencies. With the offer came a threat. The businessman investigated my friend's life and all who were assisting him, threatening professional and financial ruin if he didn't give him everything he demanded. He went on to say that if he ever found anything wrong with the house, he would hold my friend responsible and ruin him if he did not make it right.

We have been talking a lot about enemies, because David talks a lot about his enemies. With the exception of Psalm 53, every psalm between 52–64 mentions enemies. They follow an intriguing pattern: one psalm describes an enemy who is a stranger, the next portrays an enemy who is a friend or acquaintance (usually Saul), then the next presents a hostile stranger again. By this pattern, it seems that God is saying, "Some attacks will be expected, and some will be surprises." For example, David would have expected attacks from military enemies like Edom (Psalm 60), but he was surprised by Saul's hatred. Betrayal by a close friend with whom he worshiped and dined crushed him (Psalm 55), and the thought that rulers commissioned to uphold justice would collude with wickedness, disillusioned him (Psalm 58).

We can't always anticipate where attacks may come from. Someone you thought you were close to could turn against you. Someone could run your business into the ground. Someone could sue you and exhaust your resources while you are defending yourself. A disease could attack you and destroy your health. We are vulnerable people. The only thing we can do to gain peace in this life is follow David's example and run to our Savior for refuge, praising our God under the shadow of his wings.

Take Refuge (vv. 1-6)

David asks God to hear his "complaint" (v. 1). That word might sound petty to our modern ears, but in this context, it is more like a legal petition.[1] Rather than take revenge, God commands us to take injustices to him (Deuteronomy 32:35; Romans 12:19, 21). It is our only recourse against those who are secretly slandering us.

Anyone with leadership responsibilities can identify with David's plight. The higher up you are in the organizational structure, the fewer peers you have and the easier target you become. Sometimes those who follow you feel leaders have no emotions, so they freely criticize. In an instant, you can find yourself in a firestorm fueled by rumor without anyone's ever having talked to you personally. That's where David finds himself. Rather than react, he dumps all his burdens on the Lord, the same Savior you and I have.

The nature of this particular assault is "conspiracy" (v. 2, NIV). Conspiracy involves the concerted attempt to cooperate to do what is harmful or wrong. Here David's enemies have gathered together to plot how they may destroy David. These are people within David's court. Even his son conspired against him. Nothing is more painful and wounds so deeply than to be betrayed by those you know. Their weapons are not "swords" and "arrows" but words (v. 3; cf. Romans 3:13). James warns that the tongue is a deadly weapon:

> The tongue is a small part of the body, but it makes great boasts. Consider what a great forest is set on fire by a small spark. The tongue also is a fire, a world of evil among the parts of the body. It corrupts the whole person, sets the whole course of his life on fire, and is itself set on fire by hell. (James 3:5–9, NIV)

While words can be the instruments of harm, they are also the chief weapon of the Spirit's redemptive response. Later in James's epistle, he says that the words of a righteous man's prayer are powerful and effective (5:16). Solomon says that gentle words turn away wrath (Proverbs 15:1). John says those who will overcome the evil one do so by the "word of their testimony" (Revelation 12:11). When you are attacked, you can flee for refuge to God's Word and let those words combat your enemies (cf. Ephesians 6:17).

In this psalm, the surprising strategy by the enemy is exposed. First, he ambushes you (v. 4). Innocent people are not guarded; they are vulnerable. A surprise attack is usually effective because it makes the victim look guilty. An accusatory question, for instance, can be so shocking that you pause and look like you are calculating an answer to protect yourself. Walk in the security of your union with Christ. Your suffering proves your life is united to his (Matthew 5:11–12). Along with David, you are being "bruised" with Christ as his seed (Genesis 3:15), so take refuge in him. If your life is an open book to the Lord, don't be guarded or paranoid. If someone's accusation is true, even if their intent is evil, repent, seek forgiveness and thank God for the rebuke that leads you into greater faithfulness. Then move on. If your opponents are wrong, then let them fuss and fume until they extinguish themselves.

Another of the enemy's strategies is that evil people "encourage each another" (v. 5, NIV). In his sermon on this passage, Charles Spurgeon rebuked his congregation for not practicing the same strategy as the wicked: "Good men are frequently discouraged, and not unfrequently discourage one another, but the children of darkness are wise in their generation and keep their spirits up, and each one has a cheering word to say to his fellow villain."[2]

The Spirit also warns us that the wicked are secretive: "they talk about hiding their snares; they say, 'Who will see it?'" (v. 5, NIV). We must find refuge in Christ because we can never anticipate the secret plots of our enemies. Their secrecy only reflects the nature of the unredeemed human heart. The word translated "cunning" in verse 6 (NIV) is literally, "deep."[3] The human heart is a bottomless pit of ability to harm others (cf. Jeremiah 17:9; Romans 3:12–18). Ironically, while the wicked think they see in secret, "search[ing] out injustice" (v. 6), they are the ones deceived. While they perceive errors in David's life, their suspicion leads them in the wrong direction.

A pastoral word is appropriate at this point. David's heart and ours are also deep, unfathomable pits. Perhaps there is a lesson for all of us against looking too hard for the sins of others.

It is clear that our enemies are formidable. We can't confront them in our own strength—they are too numerous, too secretive, and too destructive. We can find our refuge in our Savior. What does that look like? Our enemies include our own besetting sin, cheating spouses, abusive parents, business enemies, depression, illness, and so on. While urgent measures like separation, intervention, or professional counseling may sometimes be necessary, meditation on the reality of who you are in Christ is *always* necessary. It will give you security, because you will be reminded that God cares for you so much that he sent his Son to save you. You will have peace, knowing that he is for you.

Such practices of the spiritual life will also have a profound effect on your enemies. Nothing is so powerful to transform marital conflict like a spouse who becomes immovably secure by internalizing God's promises. An emotionally unstable person can be strengthened by the faith of a friend who says to himself, "God is my refuge, what can mere man do to me?" Paul is serious when he says we have been given spiritual weapons able to destroy the devil's strongholds (2 Corinthians 10:14). The Spirit has given you the weapon of words—his Word and its promises, and the words of your effective prayers. In them, we can find refuge.

Rejoice (vv. 7-10)

This passage ends very quickly. David takes us through a thorough anatomy of evil to prepare us for the dramatic climax in verses 7–10. In this final stanza, God suddenly destroys evil with a few sharp arrows. Paul assures us that the same will happen at a cosmic level: "While people are saying, 'Peace and safety,' destruction will come on them suddenly, as labor pains on a pregnant woman, and they will not escape" (1 Thessalonians 5:3, NIV). Those who thought they were plotting evil in secrecy will be forced to realize that the God who sees was watching them and will expose their evil for all to see (Psalm 65:8). God will expose and humiliate them in such a way that those who look on will reverence God and acknowledge the justice of his works: "All people will fear; they will proclaim the works of God and ponder what he has done" (v. 9, NIV).

The Bible promises to expose evil so that all mankind will marvel. God's ways will only be fully realized in the future, when every knee shall bow and every tongue confess that Jesus is Lord (Philippians 2:10–11). It is this future promise of righting all wrongs that moved David, and must also move us, to rejoicing in the meantime.

On Christmas Eve of 1875, Ira Sankey was an unhappy man. The internationally famous gospel singer was aboard a steamer on the Delaware River heading home to Newcastle. He was worried that he might miss his train in Philadelphia and not see his family on Christmas day. He was headed home from a trip to England with the evangelist Dwight Moody, and if Moody hadn't extended their stay in England, Sankey would have been home in plenty of time. Frustrated and angry, Sankey paced the deck of the steamer as the Pennsylvania shoreline slowly passed by. Another passenger interrupted Sankey's mournful thoughts by asking him to sing. Sankey reluctantly agreed and a crowd gathered. He considered singing a couple of Christmas carols, but he felt the Lord leading him to sing this:

> Savior like a shepherd lead us,
> Much we need Thy tender care;
> In Thy pleasant pastures feed us,
> For our use Thy folds prepare:
> Blessed Jesus, blessed Jesus!
> Thou has bought us, Thine we are.

A hush fell over the crowd who slowly dispersed in a worshipful spirit. However, the silence was broken with another question, "Your name is Ira Sankey?" "Yes," answered Sankey. Out of the shadows came a man Sankey had never met. After talking for a few minutes, the two men realized they had both been in the Army in 1862, although they had been on opposite sides—Sankey on the Union side and his new acquaintance a Confederate. Not only that, they discovered they had both been in Sharpsburg the very same night, which is what prompted this man to engage Sankey in conversation:

> "I was in the Army, too. The Confederate Army. And I saw you that night." Sankey looked at him warily. "You were parading in your blue uniform. Had you in my sights, you standing there in the light of the full moon, which was right foolish of you, you know." The man paused. "Then you began to sing." Amazingly, Sankey remembered. "You sang the same song you sang tonight, Savior Like a Shepherd Lead Us. . . . My mother sang that song a lot, but I never expected no soldier to be singing it at midnight on guard duty. Especially a Union soldier." The man sighed. "Obviously I didn't shoot you."
>
> "And obviously I am grateful." Sankey smiled.
>
> "Frankly, up until tonight, the name of Ira Sankey wouldn't have meant much to me. Guess I don't read the paper like I should. I didn't know you'd turn out to be so famous!" The man smiled for the first time. "But I reckon I would have recognized the voice and the song anyplace."

As these two men chatted late into the evening, Ira Sankey said he felt the enemies of his worry and anger disappear and praise take their place.[4]

From his personal experience, David assures us that all who "take refuge in" the Lord will "rejoice" and "glory in him" (v. 10, NIV). Regardless of how the enemy has attacked you, find your refuge in Christ, and you will experience the peace that comes from knowing you are loved and protected by God.

Questions for Reflection/Discussion

1. Have you ever experienced a "surprise attack"? What was it like? What was the most distressing part of it to you (betrayal, being misunderstood, disillusionment, etc.)?

2. How does fleeing to God's Word for refuge give you peace? How does it keep you from responding in a sinful way to hurtful words or actions of others?

3. How does the final part of this psalm give us hope despite the distress we experience due to a surprise attack?

Prayer

Using the outline of this chapter, pray this psalm in your own words, asking God to give you peace as your refuge (vv. 1–6); to give you joy because of his deliverance and justice (vv. 7–10); and to give you wisdom, certainty, and the right words (or to keep you from speaking rashly) as you encounter those who attack you.

17

Backward Praise

Psalm 65

Praise is due to you, O God, in Zion.
(Psalm 65:1)

WE HAVE SEEN over the last several chapters that Jesus can give us peace even when we are overwhelmed by enemies and feelings of despair. But our Savior can and does do even more. He leads us through those experiences into true joy. Even in the midst of our suffering, he can bring us to a place where we joyfully praise him.

This psalm teaches us something important about prayer, and uses a unique strategy to do so: it appears backwards! Let me explain. For one, its theological order seems backwards. It begins with very specific praise for salvation, then moves more broadly to God's providential guidance of history, then moves most broadly to God's creation. That's not the way subjects are typically ordered in systematic theology. First, we deal with introductory matters (called prolegomena), which include an explanation of God's revelation in nature. Next, we move to the nature of God and explain how he interacts with his creation in providence. Lastly, we deal with the person of Jesus Christ and the nature of his salvation. To our finite, Western minds, it seems more logical to first prove there is a God, then show he reveals himself, and then explain that he reveals himself in order to save. If David were a professor of systematic theology in a seminary, he might have lost his position with this kind of an order!

Sometimes, orders are reversed for the sake of emphasis in order to focus one's attention on the best part. I was in a restaurant once where the dessert was brought out first. The waitress said, "Now if you order the special, this is what you get at the end." David does a similar thing. He begins with the most important topic, our salvation, and then moves backward historically. But maybe David has a pastoral purpose in ordering things as he does. Perhaps you do not even feel you can praise God. Perhaps you are even doubting your own salvation because of the lack of joy and desire to praise God. It is comforting to know that God does not require us to "rightly order" our prayers in order to be heard. We must cling to the first bit of truth we can, however small it may be, and let that result in "backward praise" of our God of grace, might, and creation.

God of Grace (vv. 1-4)

Not only does the whole psalm seem backward, this first section in itself seems backward. Some theologians describe the logic of our salvation according to the *ordo salutis*, the "order of salvation."[1] First, Christians are effectually called; then they believe and repent; then they are justified, sanctified, and adopted. Only then do we say someone is put on a course of continual sanctification and perseverance toward the goal of glorification. Part of the ongoing process of sanctification involves participating in the means of grace, which includes prayer.

David has it all backward, doesn't he? He discusses prayer in verses 1–2, justification in verse 3, and election in verse 4. I think it's because David is in the middle of a worship service, fulfilling his vows. He is offering up sacrifices of all kinds: animals, grain, hymns of praise. Perhaps he asks himself in the middle of it, "Why am I doing this?" The first answer that comes to mind is,

"Because God has answered my prayers!" Moved by that thought, he names God, the One who answers prayer (v. 2), as if to say that God is so ready to answer his children's prayers that he would deny an essential part of himself if he didn't.

That thought may then have moved David to ask, "How could God answer the prayers of a sinner like me?" The answer comes to him in verse 3: God made atonement for all his sins through his Son (Romans 3:23–26). He knew such forgiveness would demand sacrificial cleansing from God, like he had already expressed in Psalm 51. Maybe David asked, "How did that grace get to me?" If he had known the hymn, he might have sung,

> Lord, why was I a guest?
> Why was I made to hear your voice,
> and enter while there's room,
> When thousands make a wretched choice,
> and rather starve than come?[2]

The hymn answers, "love drew us in." The answer in the psalm is the same: he was chosen and brought near to be a table guest in God's house. If Christ is your Savior, then all these comforting assurances are yours.

However, some of us fail to offer thanks because we don't recognize that God has done anything particularly great for us. We may have not received anything particularly great recently because we have doubted his ability to answer prayer, and so we haven't asked. Maybe we don't ask for much because we don't really believe our sins are forgiven. Instead, rather than living as a chosen people, we live as orphans begging for bread while an overladen table of spiritual blessings is lovingly set before us to be consumed.

The way to experience again the joy of your salvation is, like David, to intentionally give thanks. Try for just one week to look for reasons to give thanks to your Savior. Refuse to complain about all that is going wrong; instead, force yourself instead to recognize the good things Christ is doing. Start with small things. If you are breathing, thank him for that. If you have a job, thank him for that. If you have a meal, thank him for that. At the end of your week, consider why you had so much to thank him for. Your answer will surely be that it is only because he loves you.

God of Might (vv. 5-8)

Such thoughts may have stirred another question in David, "How did God get heavenly salvation down to me?" The answer is that he moves heaven and earth to get it to us. Some scholars who believe the Bible is just another human book cringe at such concepts. They believe that scholars have to strip away all religious interpretations of the Old Testament to get to the real meaning. They don't believe God acted in any saving way in history; history just happens. Human history is all that counts, and somehow, God is incarnate in that history.[3]

David knows better. God *does* act in history to bring about his redemptive purposes. My friend and professor David Calhoun once preached on a somewhat obscure narrative from Joseph's life in order to relate the doctrine of providence. Here's how he explains God weaving history together to accomplish our salvation:

If Joseph had not met [a stranger in his search for his brothers (Genesis 37:15)], he would have returned home and would not have been sold into slavery; which means that he would not have become a great man in Egypt; which means that he would never have been able to provide a safe haven for his family during the famine in Israel; which means that the children of Israel would not have been persecuted in Egypt; which means that God would not have sent Moses to deliver them from the house of bondage with a strong hand and an outstretched arm and with many signs and wonders and, through forty years of desert wanderings, bring them to the land flowing with milk and honey; which means that there would have been no kingdom of Israel under Saul, and David, and Solomon, who built the temple in Jerusalem; which means that it could not have been destroyed by the Babylonians who carried away many of the people into captivity; which means that there would not have been a return to settle the hills and towns of Judea; which means that there would have been no Jewish girl named Mary by whom Jesus the Savior was born; which means that there would have been no Christianity for the apostles and others to take into all the world.[4]

Another friend of mine was teaching a Sunday school class on the conversion of Cornelius in Acts 10, when he came to verse 45 (NIV), "The circumcised believers who had come with Peter were astonished that the gift of the Holy Spirit had been poured out even on the Gentiles." One of the students yelled out, "That's me!" She realized that the unfolding story of redemption recorded in the Bible was not just how salvation came to the Gentiles long ago but also how it came to her.

Notice that the psalmist David, by inspiration of the Spirit, has in mind our salvation as he meditates on the God who is "the hope of all the ends of the earth and of the farthest seas" (v. 5, NIV). He envisions you and me, people living far away, singing songs of joy. When we think about God's power to save people to the ends of the earth, we must include ourselves, who have been reached through the missionary efforts of the church. God's mercy embraces the entire universe (Psalm 145:9; Luke 6:35), but his care extends to each of us individually as well. If you are a Christian, this is because God has engineered history from creation to the present in order to bring you to himself. You are not lost in the cosmos; you are written in God's book of life, because he wrote you into his story.

God of Creation (vv. 9–13)

Why did meditating on God's acts in history drive David to praise God for his creation? Maybe because it stirred another question, "How did God get salvation from his mind to me?" If so, he might have reasoned like this: God created the world as the stage on which he would perform his drama of redemption. Jonathan Edwards made this point in his monumental work *History of the Work of Redemption*. Edwards prioritized God's actions in history this way: the most important work is redemption in Jesus Christ, the next most important is providence, and the next is creation.[5] Then he related them this way: God created the world in order to bring redemption through Jesus Christ and victory over Satan over the course of human history. At the end of history, Edwards argues primarily from Revelation, God will not dispose of creation which served as his "house" in which to gather his family, but rather supersede it with a new creation free from all the effects of the fall just as Christians will be. Here is Edwards in his own words:

> So it ever is, then when one thing is removed by God to make way for another, the new one excels the old: tabernacle and temple; so new covenant, new dispensation: throne of Saul and David, priesthood of Aaron and priesthood of Christ, old Jerusalem and new; so old creation and new. God has used the creation that he has made to no other purpose but to subserve the design of this affair. . . . God created the world to provide a spouse and kingdom for his Son. And the setting up of the kingdom of Christ, and the spiritual marriage of the spouse to him is what the whole creation labors and travails in pain to bring to pass.[6]

One commentator described David's beautiful conclusion this way: "We venture to claim that this is the most eloquent and beautiful description of the blessings that God bestows on field and meadow to be found anywhere in such brief compass."[7] These verses make two points: First, God created the world purposefully; creation is not incidental to God's plan of redemption. Second, God created the world in order to save us.

Notice that nature is not merely dependent on God; God is actively nurturing his beloved creation. While the Bible speaks comfortably of secondary causes like the sun rising (Psalm 104:22) and the earth receiving rain (James 5:7), even these are ordained by God, the first cause of all creation: "You care for the land and water it" (v. 9, NIV).[8] God has not withdrawn from the world after creating it but instead tends and keeps it. Reflecting on these verses, Norman Wirzba says:

> God is continually in his garden creation, watering and feeding it, but also weeding and pruning it. God delights in the fruitfulness of its life, just as God expresses profound sorrow over its disease or death. God is continuously watchful and alert to the dangers that can disrupt the garden's life. God is faithful even when the garden does not produce fruit as planned.[9]

Finally, nature echoes God's grace. That awareness enhances our worship by enabling the Christian to see the gospel everywhere he or she looks in creation.

Misuse of creation is rebellion against the Redeemer. In books 1 and 2 of Augustine's *Confessions* he reviews his most heinous sins and concludes that sin is a perversion of good. Lust is a perversion of the sexual relationship God created to be good. Stealing is a perversion of work, which is good. Therefore, sin is the misuse of God's true good in creation.[10]

To live faithfully in our Father's world requires not only using its resources respectfully but also honoring God's redemptive intentions. Salvation is his most important work, history is what he crafts to accomplish it, and creation is its arena. The whole cosmos exists for him, and all of history is racing toward one goal—the praise of his glorious grace.

In her book *Life and Death in Shanghai*, Nien Chaing recounts the amazing story of her courage during Mao Zedong's revolution. She was working as an advisor for Shell Oil when Mao's officials arrested her, beat her, and put her in solitary confinement, where she remained for six years.

One afternoon while she was lying in her cell, she watched as a spider slowly climbed up the wall to the iron bars of her window. From the top of the bar it repelled down to the bottom of the bar with a silk thread. After securing that end of the thread it crawled back to where it began and swung in another direction. Nien watched with fascination as the spider created a frame and then artfully spun an intricate design inside it. She thought:

> Could it really have acquired the skill through evolution, or did God make that spider with the ability to make a web for catching food and perpetuating its species? This spider helped her to see that God was in control. From then on, Mao Tse-tung and his revolutionaries seemed much less menacing. She says, "I felt a renewal and a hope surge inside of me."[11]

That is a good pattern for the way a Christian can respond to creation. The obvious design of creation should move us to praise and trust in God, not just for the amazingness of creation but especially for his wisdom in crafting a world in which he could accomplish our salvation through Jesus Christ.

Questions for Reflection/Discussion

1. Do you ever experience times when you find it nearly impossible to even pray?

2. What does this psalm show us about having to get our prayers "right"? What does that tell you about God's love for you and his willingness to listen?

3. How does the truth of this psalm help embolden you to pray even when it feels impossible?

Prayer

This is a great psalm to learn to pray when you feel like you can't pray. Begin your prayer by focusing on just one thing (no matter how big or small) that you can thank God for. Then, reflect on who God is and what he has done. He hears your prayer (v. 2), he atones for your sin (v. 3), he is the God of your salvation, and the hope of all the ends of the earth (v. 5). Thank him for the ways he provides (vv. 9–10), and the ways the whole earth reflects his goodness (vv. 11–13). Then, consider how you can extend this thread of thankfulness to others in your circle of friends and acquaintances.

18

Come and See
What God Has Done

Psalm 66

*Come and see what God has done: he is awesome in his
deeds toward the children of man.*

(Psalm 66:5)

PSALM 65 DESCRIBED the praise all human beings owe to God
as their Creator. Psalm 66 prescribes the praise Christians owe
him as their Redeemer. We called Psalm 65 "backward praise"
because, like David, we must start with our own salvation first
before we are able to see the totality of God's work in all of creation. Psalm 66 puts our praise "back in order," so to speak. It
begins with creation and moves toward us and our redemption, nurturing in us a thankful spirit. Though that may sound
straightforward, by the Spirit's inspiration David communicates
this truth in a fresh way. Recognizing how much God has done
for us is the key to a thankful, trusting spirit.

A friend of mine once came to my office just a few days after
joining me in a new city. He was distraught. His wife was six
months pregnant; they had just traveled several hundred miles
with everything they owned in a moving van; and they were near-
ing the closing of the house they had just bought. He was emotionally exhausted, on the verge of tears, and worried sick that

somehow, something was going to go wrong with this new house, child, or city. I urged him to think about the house he was about to buy. It was old and it had many peculiarities, as old houses do. But its age also meant one other thing: it had stood the test of time. It had been well built, so that it was still standing to that day. I urged him to think about the many times throughout his life God had provided everything he needed, how God's provision for him had never broken down. Eventually, he reminded me of something God had provided for him just that week. As he reflected more and more on what God had done in his life up to that point, his worries began to dissipate. God slowly began to deliver him from his anxiety.

God has been working in your life from the time he created the universe. When you look back on what God has done in your life, it creates thankfulness and a trusting spirit that can help deliver you from worry and anxiety. In other words, what God has done can help give you peace.

God of the Creation (vv. 1–7)

David says God's handiwork is evident in what he has made (vv. 1–4). From creation, David moves on to God's providence and says that the Bible records his redemptive acts in history, so that everyone might marvel and believe (vv. 5–7). The reference to crossing the Red Sea ("He turned the sea into dry land," v. 6) and the Jordan River ("they passed through the waters on foot," v. 6, NIV) presents God's miraculous redemptive on behalf of his people Israel, which leads them to rejoice.

This is a good place to outline a few guiding principles for thinking about praise. For one, we should maintain a balance between praise and thanksgiving. Marvin Tate says that the structure of this psalm (i.e., from general to specific) illustrates how to put thankfulness into a "larger theological construct than that of purely personal concerns."[1] He means that praise focuses on God—who he is and what his larger redemptive purposes are—while prayers of thanksgiving tend to become self-consumed, concentrating on what God has done for us. Therefore, thanks must always be given with an eye to God's greater purposes. Such a prayer might sound like this:

> Thank you, Father, for healing me. You have proven not
> only that you love me, but that you love your children.
> You have not finished your work of redemption in and
> through me, but have restored me for the further expansion of your kingdom. May all who see your work in my
> life realize not only that you are my God but that you are
> the God of the universe and God of your church.

On the other hand, our praise would be empty without thanksgiving. Without concrete graces for which to give thanks, we might find ourselves offering generic praise that fails to engage our hearts. Praising and thanking God for who he is and what he has done for us go hand in hand.

We should also consider why we praise God. Is it not egotistical for God to ask people to honor him? That question bothered C. S. Lewis for some time until he understood that God deserves praise in the same sense that any work of art is admirable; that is, praise is the only proper response to a God so beautifully gracious. He also realized that God calls us to praise him because through worship we draw near to God. God does not need our worship—we do.

Praise is not something we are coerced into. We naturally praise whatever we value: a meal, a sports team, a movie. More than that, we invite others to join in. The psalmist's praise comes from the same overflow of his heart. Caught up in the wonder of God's works, David exclaims, "Come and see what God has done" (v. 5) as a child watching a parade yells, "Mommy, look!"

Add to all of this, Lewis says that praise completes the enjoyment of God's goodness.[2] Just as there is something missing when you watch a sunset alone, so praising God for his works is incomplete until we share it with the body of Christ. Somehow, telling God's people about it completes your experience of God's grace. Praising God is far from appeasing his ego; rather, it satisfies our deepest desires.

God of Might (vv. 8–12)

What David says in this section could surprise or even offend you. God is also praiseworthy because he is the God of the church and preserves her life. Keeping "our feet from slipping" (v. 9, NIV) refers both to God's literal preservation of our lives as well as the moral preservation of our character. But notice how God provided that preservation for Israel. He "tested" them (v. 10). He "refined [them] like silver" (v. 10, NIV) through prison and slavery, and caused their enemies to trample on them; he took them through "fire" and "water" (vv. 11–12).

You may feel like you are in a pressure cooker now and wonder if God is against you. If so, this psalm reminds us that God allows his children to suffer in order to refine them, like silver, and promises to "[bring] us out to a place of abundance" (v. 12).

John Calvin referred to such trials as "life under the cross."[3] If we are going to become more like Christ, then our lives must follow his pattern. That requires constant testing, so that we will transfer our trust from ourselves to Christ. David learned that truth when he wrote Psalm 30: "When I felt secure, I said, 'I will never be shaken'. . . but when you hid your face, I was dismayed" (Psalm 30:6–7, NIV). Calvin also calls suffering God's "medicine."[4] God is the heavenly physician who treats each Christian according to his disease. While some need harsher treatments than others, all are diseased with sin; therefore, none go untouched by God's healing discipline.[5] As Calvin says, suffering "marks" us as sheep of the good, suffering Shepherd.[6]

God permits hardship for many reasons. But one that the Bible returns to often is that "the LORD disciplines those he loves"

(Proverbs 3:12, NIV; cf. Hebrews 12:6). You may think trials could never be intended by God to crush your pride, root out sins of harshness, or soften your speech, but God may be turning up the heat in order to boil off indwelling sin and make you more like Jesus.

God used suffering that way in a dear friend's life. God used a derailed career, destroyed finances, a wrecked marriage, and an abscessed tooth to liberate him from alcoholism. These sufferings led him to Christ and saved his life. Alcoholism did not make him a worse sinner than others; he needed strong medicine like anyone who is diseased without Christ in their life. My friend would say with David, "I went through fire and water, but you brought me to a place of abundance" (see v. 12). With David, he urges others to join him in praising God.

God has used my own battle with depression and relationships strained by my temper to convince me over and again of my need for a Savior. While the devil can take advantage of these situations, God deserves the praise for sovereignly overruling the devil's messengers to prove the power of his grace even in our weakness (2 Corinthians 12:1–10). If you want restoration to the fullness and abundance of who you were created to be, if you want to experience heaven on earth, if you desire to be like Christ, then following in Christ's steps will include the uncomfortable but life-giving care of the divine physician.

The Bible indicates that the intensity of God's treatments will not be constant. What a relief! While weeping might last for an evening, joy comes in the morning (Psalm 30:5). He frequently urges us to be patient, which implies that something better is coming; our afflictions, however intense, are momentary (2 Corinthians 4:17). The ultimate relief will be heaven, but there are periods of relief in this life, too. Wait patiently for his medicine to work, knowing that the divine physician loves you. He is not only your doctor, but also your Father.

God of Grace (vv. 13–20)

While God is the God of creation and the church, he is also the gracious God of the individual. Astounded by thoughts of God's grace, David offers a plenitude of sacrifices: fat animals, "rams," "bulls," and "goats" (vv. 13–15). His offering was not only expensive; it was personally sacrificial. By a burnt offering, a worshiper consecrated his whole life to God in response to his mercy.

Paul followed the same pattern: "Therefore, I urge you, brothers and sisters, in view of God's mercy, to offer your bodies a living sacrifice, holy and pleasing to God—this is your true and proper worship. Do not conform to the pattern of this world, but be transformed by the renewing of your mind" (Romans 12:1–2, NIV). The only appropriate response to the grace that raises us from death to an incorruptible hope for "life . . . to the full" (John 10:10, NIV) is the total surrender of one's entire person to Christ.

Thomas Fuller said David's prayer is a wonderfully illogical syllogism:

A—God only hears the prayers of those who cherish no sin in their hearts.
> *If I had cherished sin in my heart, the Lord would not have listened;* (v. 18, NIV).
B—God heard David's prayer.
> *but God has surely listened and has heard my prayer.* (v. 19, NIV)

What would you expect the conclusion to be? David cherished no sin in his heart, right? God rewarded David's moral uprightness by answering his prayer. That's what we expect, but it is not what we get. Out of nowhere we get an intrusion of grace: "Praise be to God, who has not rejected my prayer or withheld his love from me!" (v. 20, NIV). Fuller concludes, "I looked that he should have clapped the crown on his own [but] he puts it [instead] on God's head. I will learn this excellent logic; for I like David's better than Aristotle's syllogisms, and whatsoever the premises be, I make God's glory the conclusion."[7]

God's grace through Jesus Christ is like that; it is surprising, unexpected, and invades from nowhere. But it is only surprising to the one who views things realistically. If you think you are righteous and don't need much from God, then you expect God to hear your prayers. But if you view yourself realistically as a desperate sinner, God will always surprise you with his grace.

Can you praise this God? You can if you see him as the architect of the universe, who designed it as the arena in which to redeem his people and who moves history along to accomplish your salvation. You can learn to praise him when you recognize the Great Physician lovingly administers bitter medicine to purge us from our pride in order to save our souls.

Questions for Reflection/Discussion

1. How do praise and thanksgiving work together to take us into a deeper understanding of God's purposes and provision?

2. How does this psalm reveal one possible purpose of suffering in your life? What hope do you see in verse 12 of this psalm?

3. How can our sufferings work to bring us to a fresh realization of God's grace?

Prayer

As you use this psalm to reflect on both God's work throughout the world and his specific work in you, thank him for his awesome deeds (v. 3), for his work to give life to his people (v. 9), for the way he brings his children through suffering (v. 12), and how we now get to spread word to others of his goodness (v. 16). As you think about your current needs and trials, ask God to renew your perspective based on these truths, and to encourage you through this reminder of his faithfulness.

19

The Church Is for Weaklings and Nobodies

Psalm 68:1–18

You ascended on high, leading a host
of captives in your train.
(Psalm 68:18)

FROM CHARLEMAGNE TO the French Huguenots to Oliver Cromwell to the survivors of Napoleon's assault on Moscow in 1812, this psalm has long been the most beloved among the underdog. David's prayer assures every endangered believer that God pursues us in order to protect us.[1] While the Psalms have much to teach us about emotional distress, they also show us how to live in community with one another. Psalm 68 shows us that the community called the church is one where all people must be welcome. In the same way Jesus pursues us in the midst of our distress, not after we have overcome it, the church must be a refuge. I just returned from speaking to a widows' support group in our church. Though memories of their husbands readily bring tears regardless of how long their husbands have been gone, they were having a really good time at a Christmas party. Their defiant hope and joy inspired my devotional to them. I read, "You have multiplied the nation; you have increased its joy" (Isaiah 9:3) and reminded them they are a fulfillment of Isaiah's prophecy. God has overpowered their debilitating grief by surrounding them with the church. While many around them sit in the darkness of their loneliness and devolve into self-pity, they are weekly embraced by the body of Christ. We must gratefully embrace God's genius in providing a loving community of brothers, sisters, fathers, and mothers. Given that it is made up of very imperfect people, like ourselves, it surely fails in many ways, but even with its imperfections, the church is a novel blessing in our disconnected and perfectionistic society.

Psalm 68 humbles us. It reminds us that we were weaklings and nobodies before God used his might to deal mercifully with us. It shows us that the church is exactly the place we must go to receive God's grace. Additionally, it shows us that we must "praise" him for it (vv. 4, 19, 26, NIV) by living more fully into the church's true identity as a congregation that proclaims good news to the poor and downtrodden of the world.

Protects Weaklings (vv. 1–6)

We are immediately confronted with the awesome power of God in these first two verses—power sufficient to annihilate the enemies of God's people. To God, his enemies are like smoke before wind and melting wax before fire. In language reminiscent of Moses in the Exodus, David invokes God's warrior presence. Whenever God told his people to break camp and set out, Moses would shout, "Rise up, LORD! May your enemies be scattered, may your foes flee before you" (Numbers 10:35, NIV).

The cloud was the way the Lord indicated he was going before them. It was a symbol of Immanuel—God with us—a sacramental sign that the second person of the Godhead was tabernacling in their midst for redemption (cf. Jude 5). It was the cloud, indicating the presence of a conquering Mediator, that stood between the Israelites and the pursuing Egyptian army after Pharaoh changed his mind. Exodus says that "the LORD looked down from the pillar of fire and cloud at the Egyptian army and threw it into confusion. He jammed the wheels of their chariots so that they had difficulty driving. And the Egyptians said, 'Let's get away from the Israelites! The LORD is fighting for them against Egypt'" (Exodus 14:24–25, NIV).

David is appealing for help to the same bearer of God's power, his Greater Son. God's power is never demonstrated in a vacuum; it is wielded through his Son for the sake of his people. That Christ was personally involved in the Exodus is confirmed by the "best attested reading" of Jude 5: "Though you already know all this, I want to remind you that *Jesus* [emphasis mine] delivered his people out of Egypt, but later destroyed those who did not believe."[2] That explains why his people do not cower in fear. Instead we read, "But may the righteous be glad and rejoice before God; may they be happy and joyful" (v. 3, NIV). God uses his might to act mercifully toward his people, and it causes them to celebrate. Probably thinking of the protection God provided in the past, David commands the people to "extol him who rides on the clouds" (v. 4, NIV)—an image that, for us, recalls Daniel's vision of the Son of Man who will come on the clouds to bring final judgment (Daniel 7:13; Revelation 1:7).

Next, God's protection is not merely functional but affectionate. God's people live in joy, not only because God saves their lives, but also because he nurtures them. He especially regards the weakest. Here he is described by David as a "father to the fatherless, a defender of widows," as well as the "God [who] sets the lonely in families" and "leads out the prisoners with singing" (vv. 5–6, NIV). Throughout Scripture God expresses a bias for the widow, the orphan, and the alien. For their good, he becomes exactly what each of these groups need. To the orphan who needs the strong love of a father, he becomes a father. To the widow who is at the mercy of exploiters, he becomes a defender and husband. To the lonely alien without a friend, he provides families. And to the prisoner of sin and misery, he becomes the liberator. It was this kind of ministry that would be as verifying as any miracle that Jesus was the Messiah (Luke 7:22; cf. 4:18–19).

But Jesus seldom does his work without an intermediary. He chooses instead to make such grace known through his church—that is, through people. The church is to be the existential expression of those aspects of God's love, providing spiritual restoration through evangelism, positive role models in its leadership, advocacy in its works of charity, family love in the life of the body, and liberation through its preaching ministry (1 Peter 2–3).

Some Christians try to live their life in Christ without the church. But those who cut themselves off from the community of grace end up living a parched life in a sun-scorched land. "[W]e are members one of another," says Paul (Ephesians 4:25). Those who think they are self-sufficient will eventually find themselves aching for what can only be found in God's family. They ache for a God who can steadfastly love them and dignify them with responsibility. In the absence of a community in which grace is given and received, they do not see or experience selfless compassion. They may not know the beauty of friends who rejoice with them in triumphs and weep with them in trials. If you stop for a moment and think of the benefits you have in the community of Christ, then you can also celebrate. God has flexed his muscle to carve out a place for you.

Pursues Nobodies (vv. 7–18)

The way God brings weaklings to the point that they can find protection in his church is by first pursuing them and bringing them to salvation. The stunning truth of this section of the psalm is that he pursues the nobodies of the world to become the recipients of his tender care.

Key redemptive events are highly compressed in verses 7–10; it is a montage of scenes from Israel's history, showing what God has done to pursue you and me. The first image in this slideshow is of the Israelites trekking across the desert away from Egypt:

"you, God, went out before your people, when you marched through the wilderness" (v. 7, NIV). God is protecting them from the elements during the day by covering them with the cloud and is warming them by night by his pillar of fire. He preserves their clothes from wearing out and provides bread from heaven as well as water from the rock. The next scene is at the foot of Mt. Sinai where they received the law: "the earth shook, the heavens poured down rain" (v. 8, NIV). By means of earthquakes, thunder, and lightning, God confirmed that his word to them through Moses was absolutely dependable.

These people whom God delivered from Egypt and sustained through the wilderness were headed to a land he had promised them. However, the Canaanite tribes inhabiting the land where Israel was headed were exceptionally cruel and consumed with blood and gore (Deuteronomy 9:4–5, 12:31).[3] They burnt their children as offerings and reduced their sons and daughters to temple prostitutes (Leviticus 18:20–30). They were God's creatures who despised him, despised others created in his image, and especially despised those who named his name (cf. Amos 11–12; Hebrews 11:13). Despite all this, God moved them out of the way in order to establish a people who would bring honor to his name. God moved blaspheming nations in order to build a nation through which would come his Son our Savior. More than that, he even saved some of those blasphemers (like Naaman) and harlots (like Rahab), and he continues to do so today (1 Corinthians 6:9–11).

God not only moves creation to get to his people; he not only moves nations to establish a land for his people; he also moves the spiritual realm to provide gifts for his people (v. 18). This verse is interpreted by Paul in Ephesians 4:8 to be a reference to the accomplishments of Christ for us. What would make Paul think of this verse when thinking of the work of Christ accomplished in his life, death, resurrection, and ascension? It seems likely that David wrote this psalm on the occasion of his bringing the ark back to Jerusalem. The ark, of course, represented the presence of

God; as David sees it returning to its place of rest, his mind runs back to think of all that God has done up to this point. He came down to his people and personally led them across the desert, gave them the law, defeated their enemies, and carved out a new home for them. Now he comes into the holy city to provide a centralized place of worship from which they can derive all the blessings they need for a life of godliness.

This is what moves Paul to think of Christ. He came down to our world in the incarnation and experienced full humiliation in order to identify with us and lead us out of our bondage to sin (Ephesians 4:9). But he did not stay here. After dying for our sins and rising in victory over them and defeating all our spiritual enemies, he ascended to heaven to sit at the right hand of the Father. From there he rules not only our lives, but the whole world. By means of that sovereignty, he distributes to us all the gifts that we need to be the church and accomplish its purposes. It is because of his power that bears witness to him as it works in us that we are able to carry forward his mission of serving the orphan, widow, alien, and prisoner.

Just as God gave his people the spoils of their conquered enemies in Canaan in order to accomplish the mission he had for them in that new land, so Christ gives the spoils of this world to his church to accomplish her mission. He gives gifts like ministers, teachers, elders, deacons, and counselors. He also gives money to build churches, send missionaries, and help the poor; printing presses to publish the gospel in every language and books to encourage fellow Christians; computers and the internet to take the message worldwide and facilitate encouragement of one another across great distances. Our king has captured the realms of heaven and earth to provide all the gifts we need to be the church.

In verses 15–17, we find the proof that God moves creation, nations, and the spiritual realm for the sake of nobodies. The place God chose to make his "holy hill" is a rather small mountain called Zion. It is only a few hundred feet above sea level and dwarfed by Mt. Hermon in the Bashan Range, which is nine thousand feet. Why didn't God choose a more impressive mountain? Because He chooses "the foolish things of the world to shame the wise . . . the weak things of the world to shame the strong . . . the lowly things of this world and the despised things—and the things that are not—to nullify the things that are" (1 Corinthians 1:27–28, NIV). That's what you and I were before he entered his creation to make a people for himself, leading them through the wilderness, establishing them in the Promised Land, defeating all their enemies, and bringing from them a Savior. And that Savior, born as a Jew in Bethlehem, pursued us until he made us his redeemed people. Now our King Jesus gives us all the gifts we need to be his church. This is no ordinary king. He has chosen to surround himself with a most unlikely court—orphans, widows, aliens, prisoners, poor, unwise, ignoble, and weak!

It is our family tradition to watch *Rudolph the Red Nosed Reindeer* every Christmas. A few years ago, I noticed something I had never paid attention to in thirty-four years of faithful viewing—the Island of Misfit Toys. It is the place where all misshapen, unloved and unwanted toys find refuge. Its inhabitants include toy trains with square wheels, tongue-tied talking dolls, and for a time, an elf who aspires to be a dentist and a reindeer with a red nose. I confess I always thought that was the boring part of the movie. I liked fighting the Abominable Snowman, pulling his teeth, and seeing Rudolph pull Santa's sleigh. Before, I think I always got my popcorn during the Island of Misfit Toys. That particular year, however, it struck me that the Island of Misfit Toys is ruled by a lion, just like the church. We are an organization of misfits—not many wise, not many influential, not many of noble birth—but nevertheless drawn into a distinguished community with the Lion of Judah as our King.

This reality should move us to joyful obedience. In view of such magnificent grace, is there anything our Savior cannot command us to do? With David let us say,

> Proclaim the power of God,
>> whose majesty is over Israel,
>> whose power is in the skies.
> You are awesome, O God, in your sanctuary;
>> the God of Israel gives power and strength to his
>>> people.
> Praise be to God! (vv. 34–35, NIV 1984)

Questions for Reflection/Discussion

1. Have you ever experienced the feeling that church was one of the last places you wanted to go in times of suffering/need? What was that feeling based on?

2. How does God's commitment to his church and to weak people give you hope for the grace he can extend to you through the church?

3. How can your own experience of suffering helping you make your church a place that is a refuge for other sufferers?

Prayer

As you pray, recount to God the ways he has pursued you throughout your life, to make you his child. Thank him for the way he has redeemed you, and ask him to reveal to you how you might be a part of making the church a place where the outcast, downtrodden, and marginalized feel welcome and loved.

20

The Church Made Strong

Psalm 68:19–35

Awesome is God from his sanctuary; the God of Israel—
he is the one who gives power and strength to his people.
(Psalm 68:35)

IN THE PREVIOUS chapter we saw that God does not require strength, competence, and prestige in order for us to become a part of his church. In fact, he delights to pursue the weak and obscure and empower them to accomplish his mission. However, when we engage in God's mission, we will inevitably be confronted with discouragement due to the evil that exists in the world. So how can a church full of weaklings and nobodies persevere through such circumstances? The second half of Psalm 68 shows us the hope God gives to his church as we work to fulfill his mission on earth.

This psalm gives us an occasion to look at the bigger story of Scripture. We have seen over and over throughout this book that the Psalms point to us Jesus. So what do Jesus, his church, and hope have in common?

At the end of the Bible, Jesus hosts what is known as the marriage supper of the Lamb (Revelation 21:9). This is the hope we have to look forward to as we face the trials that come with being a part of his mission. At the end, Jesus will host a feast for his church. What is a feast like for those who are invited? You are not worried. You eat peacefully because there is more than enough. And you are filled with joy as you sit in the presence of loved ones. Every earthly feast we have ever been a part of can never compare to the overwhelming peace and joy we confidently hope for when Jesus hosts us in heaven.

David predicts God will extend his church well south of Jerusalem and that someday "Envoys will come from Egypt" (v. 31). Later in redemptive history, Isaiah would prophesy God's extending his kingdom east, west, north, and south (Isaiah 43:6). Though Egypt is technically in the Northern Hemisphere, in the biblical writers' mind that city would have represented everything south of Jerusalem, as well as all of Israel's enemies. This was a bold prophecy of the power of God's grace to erase geographical, ethnic, and sociopolitical boundaries as divisions among his people. That prophecy was fulfilled as early as Acts 8:26–40 with the conversion of the Ethiopian eunuch. In recent years, Vince Bantu has introduced the Western church to the theologically robust and vibrant Christianity in Ethiopia and Egypt that existed in the first five hundred years of the last century.[1]

God continues to draw his people from all points of the compass, especially the south and east. While the growth of Christianity among northern Europeans has slowed to nearly nothing, conversions in the Global South are occurring at a staggering rate. Baylor professor Philip Jenkins is one of the leading observers of this phenomenon. Jenkins has an intriguing forecast for the growth of Christianity in the twenty-first century:

> Christianity should enjoy a worldwide boom in the new century, but the vast majority of believers will be neither white nor European, nor Euro-American. According to the respected World Christian Encyclopedia, some two billion Christians are alive today, about one-third of the planet's population. The largest single bloc, some 560 million people, is still to be found in Europe. Latin America,

though, is already close behind with 480 million. Africa has 360 million, and 313 million Asians profess Christianity. North America claims about 260 million believers. . . . If we extrapolate these figures to the year 2025, the southern predominance becomes still more marked. Assuming no great gains or losses through conversion, then there would be around 2.6 billion Christians, of whom 595 million would live in Africa, 623 million in Latin America, and 498 million in Asia. Europe, with 513 million, would have slipped to third place. Africa and Latin America would thus be in competition for the title of most Christian continent.[2]

Jenkins observes sociologically what we find expressed poetically in this psalm: God presently gives power and strength to his people, and thus assures his kingdom will triumph. That means we are on the winning side! With this in mind, in utmost confidence, we must, as David suggests, "Proclaim the power of God, whose majesty is over Israel, whose power is in the heavens" (v. 34, NIV).

God Bears Our Burdens (v. 19)

David turns from recalling the past to enumerating the present blessings that God's people enjoy. For one, God "daily bears our burdens" (v. 19, NIV). By humbling himself to put our cares and burdens on his shoulders, he proves he is the Messiah (Isaiah 46:4). This is not a new thought in the Psalter. "Cast your cares on the LORD," David says (Psalm 55:22). The promise follows: "and he will sustain you." He removes our burdens in order to embrace us.

As we engage in Christ's mission in the church, we will undoubtedly shoulder many burdens. It may be the struggles of people we are discipling. It could be the resistance of unbelievers with whom we are sharing our faith. It could be our struggles with our own sin. Or it could be feeling like we are alone in our desire for Christ's mission with seemingly no support from our peers. Whatever it is, God not only cares about it, he promises to bear that burden for us.

One fall, my dad sponsored a vacation for all of his employees (which, at the time, included me). The campsite was nestled in the woods along the river near my home. Dividing our camp from the central buildings was a slough. One night, we were walking over the bridge that spanned the slough, when our assistant manager's four-year-old son fell in the water. There were no lights on the bridge and the water was murky. All we could see was the still-lit flashlight slowly sinking to the bottom. Immediately after the little boy's splash in the water, there was a much bigger splash. It was his father. By following the flashlight, he was able to find the boy and lift him to safety. After things calmed down, my dad asked, "Paul, you don't swim. How did you know how deep it was? Didn't you think about what you were doing?"

"No," he said, "I only knew one thing: my boy was in that water."

The love of a caring father for his child paid no heed to personal risk. Here, O child of God, is his love for you.

God Gives Us Escape from Death (v. 20)

God has also provided "escape from death" (v. 20, NIV). David experienced this escape in a literal way, as God delivered him from the assaults of Saul and other enemies. David's physical salvation was a prophetic symbol of the way Christ would save us through his death, burial, and resurrection (Acts 2:29–33). Knowing that the "sting of death" (its ability to send us to hell) has been removed makes us bold witnesses. If the fear of death has been removed, then the devil's most intimidating weapon has melted in his hand. That thought is reinforced by the verb translated "escape" (v. 20, NIV). It is related to a verb in Psalm 18:19, which can be translated "he brought me forth."[3] The destination in that verse is interesting and applicable here, "he brought me forth into a broad place." By providing an escape from death, he has set our feet securely in a broad and powerful position, from which we can say to all our enemies, "In God I trust.... What can man do to me?" (Psalm 56:4, 11).

Johann Christoff Arnold, who marched with Martin Luther King, Jr. said he remembers King saying in 1963, "No man is free if he fears death. The minute you conquer the fear of death, at that moment you are free." King's friends begged him to take more precautions for his life, but he insisted: "I cannot worry about my safety," he told them. "I cannot live in fear. I have to function. If there is one fear I have conquered, it is the fear of death. I submit to you that if a man hasn't discovered something that he will die for, he isn't fit to live."[4] That is power and strength.

This promise is for us as well. God never promised that following him and engaging in his mission would be easy. In fact, he warns often in Scripture that it will be fraught with all kinds of challenges, pains, and dangers. We have this promise, however, that whatever happens to us, no one can ultimately take away eternal life. In this confidence we can face any danger.

God Promises Future Justice (vv. 21–33)

Next, the text turns from the present to the future. David prophetically describes how our power and strength will be experienced in the kingdom to come. Our power and strength will come from the ultimate victory of God's kingdom among all people; all will acknowledge, willingly or unwillingly, that God's ways are right, his judgment is just, and his grace deserves all glory.

Here and now, God comforts his children by guaranteeing future justice on all his and their enemies. This is a gory passage, but David is describing what will happen at the final judgment, not what we should expect in this life. First, those who now flaunt their power and pretend to be invincible will be crushed. Their "hairy crowns" are likely an allusion to the Middle Eastern superstition some of David's enemies may have shared, that cutting one's hair preserves strength (v. 21; cf. Deuteronomy 32:42).[5] Secondly, God promises that no matter where the wicked are—whether to the eastern fringes of Bashan or to the "depths of the sea"—he will flush them out and drag them to court on Judgment Day (v. 22; a similar description is found in Amos 9:1–3).

Finally, God promises we will participate with him in executing justice. Plunging one's feet in blood is a metaphor describing the participation of the offended parties in the act of vindication. The New Testament describes the same shared role (1 Corinthians 6:2). In Revelation 18–19, John is explicit: "Babylon," representing the secular world system and its self-worship through commercial success, its ungodliness, and its injustices, will be annihilated (Revelation 18:1–3). When that happens, God's people will be there to rejoice while the "smoke from [Babylon] goes up forever and ever" (Revelation 19:1–3). We will experience the ultimate closure of having had a hand in decimating evil (cf. Romans 16:20).

The image of dogs licking up the blood of those destroyed (v. 23) is not only an allusion to Jezebel's judgment (1 Kings 21:23), but also represents God's extermination of wickedness. There will be no end to the satisfaction among the godly that God has dealt justly with the wicked. Such assurance of justice should provide present encouragement. A world system that kills babies in the womb, steals toddlers from cars, extorts money from widows, allows and encourages racism, and hails indecency in elected officials will one day go up in smoke. Such assurance will renew our resolve to do God's will now. The harder we work for Jesus now, the more energetically we will sing in the future, "Hallelujah! Salvation and glory and power belong to our God for true and just are his judgments" (Revelation 19:1, NIV).

God Assures Us We Are Not Alone (vv. 22–35)

The final stanzas of this psalm are remarkable. David declares God will confer power and strength to us by drawing a colossal number of Jews and Gentiles from every nation on earth to worship him. It is the image of a huge processional led by singers, followed by instruments, and inclusive of all "tribes" from the north to the south and everywhere in between, including the smallest tribes like Benjamin.

So how does this future procession of praise strengthen us now? God uses numbers and geographical expanse to quell our doubts and buoy our confidence in his sovereignty. When Elijah was despondent after his conflict with the prophets of Baal, God strengthened his faith by revealing that there were seven thousand other loyal followers of God (1 Kings 18:18). When the enemy army struck fear into Elisha's servant, Elisha prayed and the Lord revealed the greater number of angelic hosts protecting his prophets (2 Kings 6:16). In Acts, Luke records the growth of the church and regularly comments, "their number increased rapidly."[6] John frequently states God's people will be an innumerable multitude from every tribe, tongue, people, and nation (Revelation 5:9; 7:9; 11:9; 13:7; 14:6).

God is always telling us that we are not alone, that we are not a part of some insignificant sect, and that our religion is not culturally bound. With indescribable delight, we will discover at the Great Day that we have so many brothers and sisters that we can't even count them. We are a part of the one people of the only God, and he has adopted his children from every people group on earth. It is easy to get discouraged now because our vision of how many Christians there are is limited. But there are a vast number of believers in the world now; thousands are being saved daily, and hundreds of millions will be gathered at the consummation of history.

This psalm makes this point clearly. As David describes Jews processing into the House of God, his mind looks forward to the day when they will process through the heavenly gates (vv. 24–27). He captures God's gathering of his Israelites by listing representative tribes from the north (Zebulun and Naphtali) and south (Benjamin and Judah). In Romans 11:26, Paul mysteriously declares, "all Israel will be saved." It will not be a small number of Israelites, because their fullness will bring "greater riches" (v. 12, NIV) and their reconciliation will be "life from the dead" (v. 15). Surprisingly, in view of the substantial rejection of the gospel by many Jews, God is not finished with ethnic Israel; he is saving many now and has designs for an even greater ingathering that will provoke worldwide revival.[7]

Jonathan Edwards believed, as did many Puritans and Christians before them, that God would save many ethnic Jews as a "visible monument of God's wonderful grace and power in their calling and conversion."[8] Likewise, David says that God will not only save a great number of Israelites, he will also save many Gentiles from every nation (vv. 28–33). That would be considered a remarkable statement among some of David's readers who tended to think grace was their exclusive possession. David, however, recognizes that God's salvation of the Jews around the world will attract Gentiles to the same hope, a hope that would later be spoken through the prophet Zechariah: "This is what the LORD Almighty says: 'In those days ten people from all languages and nations will take firm hold of one Jew by the hem of his robe and say, "Let us go with you, because we have heard that God is with you"'" (Zechariah 8:23, NIV).[9]

David mentions two nations that represent the world for him. He is probably referring to Egypt in verse 30, since he mentions it by name in verse 31. Cush (Ethiopia) was probably the most remote region known by David. The "calves of nations" (v. 30, NIV) probably refers to everyone else. From these, God will bring worshipers. Hereby he confirms to us even now that the God we worship is the only God. Though we at times feel all alone and may doubt the veracity of the message of Scripture, its message is nevertheless enduring, true, and universal, as will be finally proven by a numberless host.

In John Bunyan's *Pilgrim's Progress*, Bunyan pictures the pilgrim, named Christian, in a house owned by a man named Interpreter. It is Interpreter's job to lead him on a tour of the rooms of the house, each of which contains an allegory representing a different truth of the Christian's life. In one room there is a fireplace. In front of the fire, a man is pouring water on the fire and yet it only burns higher and hotter. The man pouring on the water represents the devil trying to extinguish the faith of a Christian.

To explain the mysterious fire, Interpreter takes Christian behind the wall and shows him a man pouring oil on the same fire.[10] That man, of course, is Christ, who powerfully strengthens the faith of the Christian against the devil's attacks. From this passage, we understand that his oil includes the bearing of our burdens, escape from death, promise of future justice, and assurance of a great host of fellow worshipers. Interpreter finally explains why Christ is standing behind the wall. It is because our trials often obscure our vision of him. Passages like this bring us behind the wall and reveal him afresh to our eyes, explaining why the flame of our faith, while it at times burns low, is never extinguished. God graciously pursues weaklings and nobodies into his church and he upholds them through the strength of his son.

Questions for Reflection/Discussion

1. What discouragements do you face with regard to being part of God's mission?

2. What promises are revealed in this psalm regarding what God does for his people?

3. How does Jesus prove that God can accomplish his mission by using what looks like weakness?

Prayer

Praying this psalm can help us admit our need for God and relinquish control to him. Ponder on each section of the psalm, asking God to renew your trust in him, give you joy in light of the way he makes his church strong, and to show you how he can use you to a part of his work.

- God bears our burdens (v. 19).
- God gives us escape from death (v. 20).
- God promises future justice (vv. 21–33).
- God promises us we are not alone (vv. 22–35).

21

Life under the Cross

Psalm 70

You are my help and my deliverer; O LORD, do not delay!
(Psalm 70:5)

THROUGHOUT THIS BOOK, we have seen again and again through the Psalms what Christ does for us. There are a few Psalms, however, that point even more clearly to Christ than others. This psalm is one of them. Like Psalm 40, it is not only predictive of the work of Christ; it records the very words of Christ. Psalm 40:6–7 is quoted in Hebrews 10:5–7 and attributed to Christ: "Sacrifice and offering you did not desire, but a body you prepared for me; with burnt offerings and sin offerings you were not pleased." That is curious, because there is no record of his having spoken those words in his earthly ministry. Apparently, the writer to the Hebrews read these verses in Psalm 40 as the words of Jesus spoken through David. By the Holy Spirit, he understood these words to be descriptive of what Jesus would endure for us.

Andrew Bonar said, "Now, in the early ages, men full of the thoughts of Christ, could never read the Psalms without being reminded of their Lord."[1] Reading these words, we cannot help but appreciate that Christ experienced everything conceivable in order to be our perfect substitute. When you read the Psalms, you should grow in your confidence that Christ, by uniting himself to you, took up all of your infirmities and carried all your sorrows (Isaiah 53:4–6). Augustine said,

> It is His voice which ought by this time to be perfectly known, and perfectly familiar, to us, in all the Psalms; now chanting joyously, now sorrowing; now rejoicing in hope, now sighing at its actual state, even as if it were our own. We need not then dwell long on pointing out to you, who is the speaker here: let each one of us be a member of Christ's Body; and he will be speaker here.[2]

What does all this mean for you? It means that as you read the Psalms from beginning to end you find a God-authored script by which to confess every category of human suffering or sinful temptation. That record should encourage you that Christ experienced it all on your behalf. That is, Christ's union with our lives not only means that he experienced everything we will experience, it also means that we will share his experience as well. This psalm shows us why that is and how we should respond.

When I was learning how to play basketball in grade school, I went to a camp sponsored by C. M. Newton, the head coach at the University of Alabama. Every day he would bring in one of his star players who went on to play in the NBA. I was so excited to see them because I just knew that in this week they were going to teach me to dribble between my legs, pass behind my back, and dunk just like they did. I was disappointed at first, as they made us dribble for a minute with our right hand, then with our left, then back and forth between the two. I was irritated at having to practice the fundamental shots over and over: twenty-five layups, twenty-five short set shots, twenty-five foul shots. Finally, I expressed my frustration to my coach, who was once a star himself. He very wisely answered me, "Son, we didn't get to be where we are without doing what you're doing now." If I wanted to be like my coach, I had to repeat the pattern of his career. I could not experience his glory until I was trained.

In the same way, we must follow the pattern of Christ's life if we will share his same glory (see 2 Corinthians 1:5; Philippians 1:21). Jesus ensures that all who trust him for salvation follow in his steps. He unites our lives to his to guarantee that ours follow his. Accordingly, the sufferings that we experience in this life equip us to experience glory. Christ's words in this psalm record the direction of the Christian life: suffering, supplication, and surrender. As these were the marks of Christ's life, they must be yours as well.

Suffering (vv. 1–3)

God's providence will bring suffering into your life. At the opening of John Calvin's book on the Christian life, he writes: "For whomever the Lord has adopted and deemed worthy of his fellowship ought to prepare themselves for a hard, toilsome, and unquiet life, crammed with very many and various kinds of evil."[3] That is what the Christian life promises (John 16:33; Philippians 3:10). However, there is nothing we will experience that God did not first put his Son through. If we are going to be reshaped from the children of evil into the children of God, some painful correctives will be necessary.

Fear is the most obvious trial described in these verses. To reinforce how afraid he was, David gets straight to the point: "Make haste, O God, to deliver me; O LORD, make haste to help me!" (v. 1). In other words, "the case required speed."[4] This compact prayer only reinforces the desperate shuddering fear of the Savior in the garden. You have surely known such fear. Maybe you are experiencing it now. It may be the anticipation of job loss, a dreadful diagnosis, a collapsing economy, or a seemingly hopeless political situation. While it may not look exactly like the Savior's fear, it is the same category. You are following in his steps, becoming like him in carrying some measure of the weight of the world.

Next, David describes himself as one whose life is in danger, citing "those who want to take [his] life" (v. 2, NIV). Like the Jewish religious leaders and Roman officials hunting Jesus, David's enemies "desire his ruin" (v. 2, NIV). Threats against your life can provoke you to desperate measures. Our Savior knew desperation. You may be experiencing such threats now: coworkers laying traps to bring you down, family members pursuing your ruin, gossip from close friends, or business challenges that threaten your livelihood. You are following in the Savior's threatened steps.

Then our Savior is mocked. We hear it in the "Aha"s—the jeers of the passersby who said, "He saved others, he cannot save himself" (Matthew 27:42). He was a humiliated man. Perhaps someone is mocking you, too. Your spouse has left you and people are taunting you, "So what good is that faith doing you now?" Or you are depressed and your own misery stabs at you: "Where is that joy, joy, joy, joy down in my heart?" You are walking in the Savior's mocked steps. The Bible gives us good reasons why walking in the Savior's steps carries a much greater purpose.

Trust. Walking with Jesus through threat provokes us to trust. If we were never humbled, we would never trust God. David confesses God had to save him from delusion: "When I felt secure, I said, 'I will never be shaken' . . . but when you hid your face, I was dismayed" (Psalm 30:6–7, NIV). There are times when God allows trials to force us to trust him at all times. Trials have a way of producing true Christlikeness, because they force us to live under Jesus's lordship. They force us to see reality.

David is most true to who he is when he is under attack. His spiritual insight is clearest when he's desperate for God. But when his borders are secure, he trusts in himself and grows arrogant. Moses prophesied that his would in fact be Israel's pattern: "Jeshurun grew fat and kicked; filled with food, he became heavy and sleek. He abandoned the God who made him and rejected the Rock his Savior" (Deuteronomy 32:15, NIV). If we are comfortable, we must live in a posture of repentant trust so that we do not wander but remain steadfast—so that when trials do come, we will be poised to see God's purposes more clearly.

Experience. Trials also provide occasion for us to experience God's faithfulness right now, in our current struggle (2 Corinthians 1:4). Without the experience of trouble, we would never know his comfort. And without the experience of comfort, we would not know his faithfulness. And if we never experienced his faithfulness to his promises, we would never truly believe he is God. God proves himself existentially, in part, by allowing us to go through trials.

Proof. Finally, endurance of truly painful trials proves the reality of the faith God has placed in us. We are not stoics; trials are truly painful. Jesus taught this by his words as well as his example. Jesus wept over the pain he saw in his friends and over what he experienced himself. The fire of our trials has to be hot so that, when we pass through to the other side, God can show our faith to be more enduring than gold. Only the faith that passes this kind of testing will be proved genuine and "result in praise, glory and honor when Jesus Christ is revealed" (1 Peter 1:7, NIV).

Supplication (vv. 2–4)

Perhaps you have learned the ACTS pattern for prayer: Adoration, Confession, Thanksgiving, Supplication. It is designed to lead us through the gospel each time we pray. However, to follow Jesus's pattern of supplication while suffering, we will depart from this pattern. At times, both Jesus and David did not wait to ask for God's help. There are times when the situation is so desperate that we must flee directly to God. Charles Spurgeon provided this encouraging comment about hasty prayers:

> I believe it is very suitable to some people of a peculiar temperament who could not pray for a long time to save their lives. Their minds are rapid and quick. Well dear friends, time is not an element in the business. God does not hear us because of the length of our prayer, but

because of the sincerity of it. Prayer is not to be measured by the yard or weighed by the pound. It is the might and force of it, the truth and reality of it, the energy and intensity of it. You who are either of so little a mind or of so quick a mind that you cannot use many words or continue long to think of one thing, it should be your comfort that exclamatory prayers are acceptable. Moreover, it may be, dear friend that you are in a condition of body in which you cannot pray any other way. A headache such as some people are frequently affected with for the major part of their lives—a state of body that the physician can explain to you—might prevent the mind from concentrating itself long on one subject. Then, it is refreshing to be able repeatedly and again—fifty or a hundred times a day—to address one's self to God in short, quick sentences, the soul being all on fire. This is a blessed style of praying.[5]

God is not so distant that he refuses to hear prayers that do not follow a certain pattern. He gives us grace by hearing and responding to all of our prayers.

Christ also prays for his enemies (vv. 2–3). Ultimately, Christ prayed this in his suffering. If it had only been David's prayer, we might judge him to be petty and vengeful. But when we see them as Jesus's words, we learn how to pray that wicked schemes would be halted. We must not only pray for our own safety; we must also mercifully pray that their plans would be thwarted.

Dan Allender gives advice for dealing with the ordinary sinner, the fool, and the evil person. An evil person is one whose conscience is seared so that he hurts people without blinking an eye. Allender says we must give such a person "the gift of defeat." That is, you must set up whatever boundaries you can to stop his assault, like refusing to talk if he is abusive. More importantly, you must pray that God would put roadblocks in his way that would "give him the gift of defeat" and lead him to repentance.[6] Obviously, Christ's prayer was answered in the centurion who believed (Acts 10) and Paul who was converted (Acts 9).

Notice how Christ lifts his eyes above his own situation to pray for all the godly who suffer: "But may all who seek you rejoice and be glad in you; may those who long for your saving help always say, 'The LORD is great!'" (v. 4, NIV). He is praying for us and the sufferings we will encounter. By praying that we could someday exclaim, "The LORD is great!" he asks that our faith would triumph. This is a prayer for a faith like Job's. After Job heard that all his possessions had been destroyed and his sons and daughters had been killed, he said,

> Naked I came from my mother's womb,
>   and naked I will depart.
> The LORD gave and the LORD has taken away;
>   may the name of the LORD be praised.
>   (Job 1:20–21, NIV)

There is only one way a person can express such faith: it is a gift from God. What a comfort to know Christ prays for our faith and God answers. We must pray the same for one another, asking that God would be strong in our fellow believers.

I remember how, as a young pastor, I once saw this strength in a dear prayer warrior. From any outsider's perspective, she had a sad life. She was all alone—never married and estranged from her siblings. Her existence appeared bleak. But you would never know it from her way of life. She had a contagious joy and used her freedom to advance the kingdom worldwide through prayer. In view of her sufferings, she once asked me, "Why do you think I have a sense of humor?"

"Because God is strong in you?" I guessed.

"Exactly!" she said.

Surrender (vv. 4–5)

Finally, the Savior humbly exemplifies that one cannot even make supplication until he is surrendered to God's will. The tension between the petitions, "God is great!" and "I am poor and needy" illustrates what Calvin calls the "contradicted soul."[7] That is, we always have contradicting desires in our souls. On the one hand, when we meet trials, we wish to flee from them, cave in, and even abandon the faith. On the other hand, because the Spirit of Christ dwells in us, we resist those urges.

The believer recognizes that he has this conflict in his soul. He cannot rejoice in trial, be glad in tribulation, or desire God's glory in affliction unless God helps him. As counterintuitive as it sounds, the Christian triumphs when he acknowledges he is helpless. That is why Jesus said in the Beatitudes, "Blessed are the poor in spirit, for theirs is the kingdom of heaven" (Matthew 5:3). Contrary to popular opinion, God does not help those who help themselves; God helps those who recognize they *can't* help themselves. We will not keep the faith unless God enables us. So ask him not only to preserve you but also to cause you to rejoice. Then pray that God would bring glory to his name by showing others how his strength undergirds your overcoming faith.

Finally, Christ teaches us to pray for his coming, even as he prayed in Gethsemane for God to come near to him and rescue him from his suffering. Evidence of a surrendered spirit is one's confidence in the second coming of Christ. When your trials mount up, when you lose treasured possessions, when broken relationships surround you, when the grotesque evils of the world threaten to engulf you, you can cast your eyes forward to the promise that Christ is coming someday to cure the world. If you are not living with a consciousness of Christ's appearing, then you will always be lured toward fleeing discomfort, denying the reality of sin, or growing cynical in the face of a world that still needs to be redeemed.

God urges you to pray, "Come, Lord!" (1 Corinthians 16:22, NIV). In the last chapter of Revelation, Jesus promises three times, "I am coming soon" (Revelation 22:7, 12, 20). Even after the third and most emphatic assurance, "Yes, I am coming soon," John shouts, "Amen. Come, Lord Jesus!" By constantly praying for him to come, we acknowledge that only he can cure our ills.

I once heard Joseph Stowell, then president of Moody Bible Institute, relate a conversation he had with the director of the Shepherd's Home for children with Down Syndrome. The director asked, "Joe, do you know what our biggest maintenance problem is?"

Stowell answered, "No, I couldn't guess."

"Dirty windows," the director answered. He then explained, "We teach our kids that Jesus came, Jesus died for sins . . . and someday Jesus will return through the clouds in the eastern sky to make us whole. Our biggest maintenance problem is fingerprints on the windows—kids looking for Jesus to come."[8]

Our lives should be filled with dirty windows, too. They should bear our fingerprints from looking for him and praying, "Come, Lord Jesus." Jesus responds, "Yes, I am coming soon."

Questions for Reflection/Discussion

1. How is Jesus revealed in this psalm?

2. If Jesus gives us the Psalms to pray to him in times of distress, what does that tell you about his willingness to bear with us?

3. This psalm assures us that suffering is evidence of our union with Christ. How can that give you peace? How can it give you hope?

Prayer

Thank God for the example of Jesus and the trust he displayed in his Heavenly Father in his suffering, supplication, and surrender. Thank him for his promise to be with you in your own struggles and hardships, and ask him to give you peace in the midst of them.

22

The Real World

Psalm 73

*My flesh and my heart may fail, but God is the strength
of my heart and my portion forever.*
(Psalm 73:26)

HOW DO YOU deal with the disturbing inequities around you?
Do you deny them? Are you tempted to deny your faith? Are you
tempted to reshape your faith to fit the disturbing realities you
notice? Perhaps another way to ask it is: What is the real world? Is
it based only on our perception based on present realities, or is it
based on something else?

It is tempting to shape our idea of the real world based on
circumstances, especially when they cause us pain or confusion.
Edmund Clowney said, "Our deepest needs drive us to our deepest beliefs."[1] The psalmist Asaph gives us a healthy pattern for
diving into the ugly waters of this world and emerging an even
stronger believer.

Psalm 70 showed us that Jesus connects himself to us in every
part of our human experience. This means that we can face the
sometimes harsh realities of this life with hope, knowing that we
are united to a Savior who brings us through them. Psalm 73 is
perhaps the greatest biblical example of this. Based on what we
observe from this psalm, it seems Asaph was a very godly, careful, thoughtful man. In other words, he dared to gaze into the

harshest realities of the world to the point that he was shaken a bit in his faith. However, he was anchored to what he knew to be true about God, so he recovered to be even stronger than he was at first.

The real world is the way God sees it, not how you and I interpret it. Our calling as Christians living under the lordship of Christ is to draw near to him so that we can see the world the way he sees it. It is exactly what this passage calls us to do. This passage will only reinforce to you that to do so is a gracious thing, because God is good and it is a blessing to live life from his perspective. God's Word shows us that viewing the real world from God's perspective may follow the pattern Asaph follows in this passage. He begins with a complaint; he is eventually corrected; and he ends by fleeing to Christ as his "refuge" (v. 28).

Complaint (vv. 2–14)

It might sound strange to you that I would say that arriving at an accurate perspective of the world includes complaint, but I think if the Psalter teaches us anything, it is that we can and should ask God the big questions, even if they include doubts, questions, or anger. There is safety with God in doing so. He is big enough to take them. I think the Bible encourages us to ask them because the Spirit knows that it is the avenue to a strengthened faith, a larger vision of God, and an accurate view of the world.

Against the Wicked (vv. 2–12)

Asaph first complains to God about the inequities he perceives in regard to the conduct of the wicked. They seem to experience none of the pain that he endures while they get everything they want. Asaph's complaints about the wicked are so honest that they are worth repeating at length:

> They have no struggles;
> > their bodies are healthy and strong.

They are free from common human burdens;
    they are not plagued by human ills.
Therefore pride is their necklace;
    they clothe themselves with violence.
From their callous hearts comes iniquity;
    their evil imaginations have no limits.
They scoff, and speak with malice;
    with arrogance they threaten oppression.
Their mouths lay claim to heaven,
    and their tongues take possession of the earth.
Therefore their people turn to them
    and drink up waters in abundance.
They say, "How would God know?
    Does the Most High know anything?"
This is what the wicked are like—
    always free of care, they go on amassing wealth.
        (vv. 4–12)

Perhaps Asaph's complaints resonate with you. Notice how Asaph categorizes them.

No Suffering (vv. 4–5): For one, they seem to have better health than those who do right. Have you seen this play out? A cruel husband outlives his godly wife. While you battle one illness after another and are in danger of losing your job, your self-serving boss enjoys a healthy life and more and more bonuses.

No Consequences (vv. 6–8; 11–12): Furthermore, they never seem to suffer any consequences for their wrongdoing. I'm sure you can relate. It sometimes seems as though you could park one time in an illegal spot and get a ticket, while they could steal the police car and never get caught. Ungodly politicians seem to be immune to troubles. They claim that no one will catch them, not even God. More than that, they seem to be right. Not only do they not suffer, but they seem to get everything, even blessings.

Heaven (v. 9): They are prominent members of their churches, giving public testimony about their heavenly inheritance.

Earth (v. 10): As a consequence of their public persona, people flock to them. People want to follow ones who are so successful in a material way while maintaining a public spiritual life.

Against God (vv. 13–14)

That perspective naturally leads to accusation of God. Asaph comes to believe that God is actually turning a blind eye to what the wicked do and is carelessly allowing his child to flounder. Therefore, in view of the prosperity of the wicked and his own difficulty relative to theirs, Asaph begins to complain that he has "kept [his] heart pure" "in vain" (v. 13).

In fact, Asaph concludes, there is no benefit because there is no justice with God. God obviously rewards the wicked and punishes the righteous. Asaph can see no redeeming purpose in his suffering. He concludes that it is punishment from a God who has changed all the rules so that now he rewards evil and punishes good. As Asaph writes, his bitterness seems to grow. Does that sound familiar to you? I think we can all admit that we have struggled with the same realities that are troubling Asaph.

Notice that God allows him to express his complaint. God says nothing against him and does nothing to hurt him. There is safety with God to express this kind of complaint. By such forbearance, the God of mercy was already preparing his people for a "priest who is [able] to sympathize with [their] weaknesses," the one we know as our Savior (Hebrews 4:15). If you belong to Christ, you are held securely by God's love. You can take your complaints to him without getting lost or hurt. God loves you so much that he is willing to allow you to express your frustrations, knowing that it will ultimately take you into a deeper understanding of who he is.

Correction (vv. 1, 15–20)

Once you have poured out your concerns to God, prepare to be corrected. The "Lord disciplines" those he loves, even as his Son endured all discipline to be our perfect Savior (Hebrews 12:6). In anticipation of that disciplining process in Christ, Asaph relates the process he experienced.

Renewal of Perspective (vv. 15–17)

In times of doubt we need a transcendent perspective. As long as Asaph tried to make sense of things by his own reasoning, he was deeply "troubled" (v. 16, NIV). It was not until he worshiped—"till I entered the sanctuary of God" (v. 17, NIV)— that his perspective was renewed by God's Word and he was able to see clearly again.

We are no different. This whole world and our flesh are drawn up against truth. The different forms of media that confront you every day, all day, constantly shout a pagan worldview at you: "live for yourself." Perhaps you work in a business structure which constantly preaches, "It's all about money." Your own heart regularly whispers, "God is not fair." But when you open the Bible in your private worship, or sit under its instruction in corporate worship, your eyes are refocused on what is real.

Because untruth resonates with who we are more naturally than truth, we can live comfortably in it for a very long time. God's perspective of the world is foreign and unnatural to us, so we don't feel like we are missing anything. That is why studying the Bible and going to church can be so difficult; it is a stretching, straining, sometimes painful exercise. I remember when the first of my friends got glasses in the third grade. He was absolutely amazed that trees had leaves. For years he had believed that trees wore a sort of wig. If you had told him before glasses that trees had individual leaves, he would have laughed and insisted that his perspective was right; and he was perfectly content with it. But when his glasses revealed to him that he was wrong and the truth was that trees contain beautiful individual decorations called leaves, he was thrilled with the new revelation. You may be perfectly content in a false view of the world, but even if you are not miserable does not mean that you can't be indescribably happier by seeing things God's way.

Destruction of Wicked (vv. 18-20)

For Asaph, the main corrective lens he needed was that which helped him see the destiny of those who spurn God in this life: "then I understood their final destiny," he says (v. 17, NIV). In the midst of the worship service he remembered that unbelievers will upon death be separated from God and suffer torment in hell. Those who ignore God may prosper in this brief life, but they will suffer eternally. If you are a believer, you may suffer for a brief time, but you will ultimately live in joy forever. Matthew Henry said, "All is well that ends well, everlastingly well; but nothing is well that ends ill, everlastingly ill."[2]

Devotion of God (v. 1)

I have delayed commenting on verse 1 until now, because it helps us understand how Asaph was corrected so readily. "Surely God is good to Israel," he says, "to those who are pure in heart" (v. 1, NIV). Asaph entered his doubts believingly. The psalm begins with this firm declaration that God is good to his people, to those whose hearts have been made pure by his grace. With that firmly fixed in his mind, he explores his doubts.

The first time I went rappelling, I was a bit nervous. But the idea that the rope holding me was attached to a tree that had not moved in several decades was very comforting. I might slip, but the tree and rope would keep me from falling. The psalmist attached his rope of faith onto the truth that God is good, and then and only then does he inch down into the abyss of doubt.

Confession (vv. 21–28)

After God renews Asaph's perspective, Asaph acknowledges his error and confesses it to God: "When my heart was grieved and my spirit embittered, I was senseless and ignorant; I was a brute beast before you" (vv. 21–22, NIV). Asaph confesses because in his heart of hearts he envied the material blessings of the wicked, coveting that which God had not given him. Furthermore, Asaph's complaints reveal that he forgot the benefits that were his as a child of God. In verses 21–28 he recounts those blessings just as quickly as he voiced his complaints.

Presence of God (vv. 23, 28): "Yet I am always with you; you hold me by my right hand" (v. 23, NIV). Asaph's acknowledgement of the presence of God is a profession of belief in Jesus. Immanuel—God with us—has come in the flesh and remains with us by means of his Spirit. You have the very presence of God. He has made your body his temple. He says there is no place in the universe you can go without him. He promises to be with you to the end of the age. By his Spirit he bears witness to your conscience that you are a child of God. You cannot take that blessing for granted. Asaph concludes that "it is good to be near God" (v. 28, NIV).

God's Word (v. 24): "You guide me with your counsel." Christ ministers his perfect presence to you by means of the Word which he brings to life in you. You have God's Word, which shows you the way to a joyful life. Look around you at the misery, chaos, and turmoil of those who do not have the clear direction of God's Word.

Advocacy (v. 25): "Whom have I in heaven but you?" We also have an advocate in heaven. "If God is for us, who can be against us? . . . Who shall bring any charge against God's elect?" (Romans 8:31, 33). We have been justified by Christ. No one else's verdict ultimately matters.

Eternal Life (vv. 26–27): "My flesh and my heart may fail, but God is the strength of my heart and my portion forever." Greatest of all, we will never die. There is nothing that we will lose on earth that we will not regain many times over in heaven. Like Asaph, when we confess our sins, we are able to return to a state of thanksgiving for God's indescribable gifts to us in Christ Jesus.

Recently, the title of a collection of essays caught my attention, *Marriage: The Dream That Refuses to Die*. Known as "Betsy" to her friends, Dr. Elizabeth Fox-Genovese was a professor of humanities at Emory University for many years; she passed away in 2007. She had the distinction of founding the first women's studies program in the country. She and her colleagues in the women's studies program were known in academic circles as "reasonable Marxists." For many years she taught her courses from an atheistic and Marxist perspective. Reflecting on her childhood, Fox-Genovese characterized her family as "non-believing Christians." By that she meant that they were generally respectful of Christianity's moral underpinnings but never went to church and never professed Jesus "as personal savior or Lord." She explained that by the time she finished college and graduate school, she had thoroughly embraced the atheistic perspective of her professors.

However, in 1995 she converted to Christianity, a story she described in the magazine *First Things* a few years before her death.[3] This text reminds me of her story because she explained that it was viewing the tragic end of unbelief that drove her to Christ. Asaph was already a believer, but both he and Dr. Fox-Genovese saw the same end and were driven to the same place after beholding its horror.

Specifically, Fox-Genovese had been thinking and writing about the importance of legalizing abortion so that women could "develop their talents." However, the more she and her colleagues espoused moral relativism of the right of every individual to determine what is right and wrong, the more frightened she became about the inevitable result. She concluded:

> It seemed difficult to imagine a world in which each followed his or her personal moral compass, if only because the morality of some was bound, sooner or later, to clash with the morality of others. And without some semblance of a common standard, those clashes were more than likely to end in one or another form of violence.[4]

She saw abortion as one form of that violence—one person deciding that another did not have the right to live. Such violence would eventually lead to assisted suicide and genocide. As the horrific end of unbelief sank in on her, she understood that the lordship of Christ was the only way to true life. Gradually she came to affirm her personal faith in Christ as Lord and Savior.

With God's Word close by, look into the abyss of unbelief; God will go with you. Tell him what you think and how you feel. He will not abandon you in your doubts; he will reveal to you the many benefits that are yours as a child of God.

Questions for Reflection/Discussion

1. Do you ever find yourself reluctant to face disturbing or difficult realities? What do you think contributes to this reluctance? Do you ever find yourself reluctant to pray as honestly as Asaph does in this psalm? Why or why not?

2. How does the resolution of this psalm show us we can approach God honestly? How does it instruct us to approach God humbly?

3. How does Asaph experience peace, hope, and joy in this psalm? How does this embolden you to go to God honestly in the face of difficult realities you face?

Prayer

Just like Psalm 23 and 51, this is a great psalm to learn how to pray regularly. It teaches us how to be honest with God and allow him to renew our perspective on the circumstances in our lives.

- Pray through verses 1–17 of this psalm in your own words, being honest with God about any particular circumstance in your own life that is causing your frustration or confusion. What difficult situation are you struggling to understand?
- Examine verses 18–28, and ask God to renew your perspective, remembering how he will one day make all things right and bring you to be with himself, and that he has you safe in his hands right now. Ask for the strength he promises as you make him your refuge.

23

What to Do with Anger

Psalms 129, 137, 140

*I know that the LORD will maintain the cause of the afflicted,
and will execute justice for the needy.*

(Psalm 140:12)

THINK ABOUT PSALM 73 with me for a moment. In one sense, Asaph's perspective needed to be realigned. God was gracious to do so for him. In another sense, there was an anger in his tone that was right. He was angry that those who do not honor God seem to live lives free from hardship. Meanwhile, the righteous were suffering.

Anger can be a very complicated emotion. The three psalms in this chapter help us process our anger and respond righteously rather than destructively. This is important, because although our anger is often directed at something or someone, it actually is destroying us. It steals our peace, because we convince ourselves that we cannot be at peace until whatever it is that has made us angry is resolved. It steals our hope, because it reminds us that we cannot control everything as we sometimes wish we would. And it steals our joy, because no one can be joyful with clinched jaws and fists.

What is it that makes you angry more than anything else? Perhaps you have been taught that all anger is sinful. Therefore, when you become angry, you are torn between the real feelings of anger and the thought that you should not be angry in the first place! It can be terribly frustrating. However, these three psalms demonstrate to us that there is a place for anger in the Christian life. In fact, these three psalms are imprecatory prayers, voicing an anger rightly kindled against all deviations from God's will in this world. As such, they provide a divinely inspired script for us on such occasions.

I have a very tenderhearted wife. In our many years of marriage she has taught me volumes about the mercy of God. She has a great sense of justice for the downtrodden in society. Recently, she was reading about some issue—I think it was some scam pulled on elderly women—and her ire was rising. These were weak people whom it appeared could not get earthly justice. Finally, she exclaimed, "We need to pray one of those imprecatory psalms you have preached about!"

In these psalms, God provides the vocabulary we need to pray against the injustices of this world, those who work against his kingdom causes. They liberate us from anxious helplessness and connect us to true power. This is what we are praying for in the second request of the Lord's Prayer, "Thy kingdom come." In asking for Christ's kingdom to come, we are petitioning that all other competing kingdoms will fail and ultimately be destroyed in the judgment.

When to Pray

God's people are created for worship. Whenever they are impeded in their worship, these prayers should be prayed. The psalmist painfully recalls what the Babylonians required the Israelites to do while in captivity: "There on the poplars we hung our harps, for there our captors asked us for songs, our tormentors demanded songs of joy; they said, 'Sing us one of the songs of Zion!'" (Psalm 137:2–3, NIV). Because these verbs are in the perfect or past tense, some think the author of Psalm 137 is a Levite who just returned to Jerusalem from Nebuchadnezzar's

Babylonian captivity.[1] He is distressed because God's worship has been impeded due to both Israel's sin and Babylon's destruction of the temple; he is not just venting his personal disappointment. He asks, "How can we sing the songs of the LORD while in a foreign land?" (v. 4, NIV). When true worship is being hindered, we should pray God would do what is necessary to restore it. In Psalm 140, David's ultimate concern is for his people to be preserved in order to fulfill their God-ordained purpose: praising the Lord (Psalm 140:13, cf. Psalm 88).

We should also pray when God's church, his treasured possession, is suffering harm. In Psalms 129 and 140 the psalmists are complaining against the humiliating abuse of Israel. The history of Israel had seen perennial instability and suffering from the beginning (from their "youth," 129:2). Their persistent humiliation is captured by the image of plowing the back (129:3, cf. Isaiah 51:23). The book of Revelation explains why Israel experienced such mistreatment through history; it is because the Messiah has come through Israel (Revelation 12:2, 13). At the dawn of redemptive history God told Adam and Eve to anticipate a perpetual, cosmic and historic battle in which Satan would attempt to destroy the human line through which the Messiah would come (Genesis 3:15). Not only did God preserve Jesus's ancestry; the Bible indicates he plans revival among the Jews that will in turn spark a worldwide ingathering of all ethnicities (Romans 11:11–12, 25–26). The protection of his covenant people in order to bring the Messiah is a confirming sign of God's intent to preserve all his covenant people, including Gentiles grafted into Abraham's line by faith in the same Messiah (Romans 11:17; Galatians 3:6–8). Therefore, when we read about the systematic persecution of the church of Jesus Christ in places like Sudan, Vietnam, and Pakistan, we can pray with hope God would do what it takes to preserve them.

It is also appropriate to pray these prayers when wicked people put up barriers to stop the progress of the gospel. David wrote Psalm 140, and his concerns were for the chosen kingdom he ruled over, which he recognized as the typological rule of Christ. We know by his own example that he was not interested in personal vengeance, because when he had the opportunity to kill Saul, his main tormentor, he refused to take matters into his own hands (1 Samuel 24:10, 26). Therefore, his complaint about slanderous speech was not just because his feelings were hurt. Yes, he was concerned about his people. He knew that untruthful speech in his court could spell the deaths of many innocent people (Psalm 140:3). Likewise, if he were destroyed in a trap, it could destabilize his whole nation and make the existence of God's chosen people insecure (vv. 1-2, 4-5). But the greater reason for his concern was that if he and his kingdom were destroyed, there would be no greater Son of David to accomplish salvation—Jesus Christ.

So, what does it look like to be concerned about attacks on God's kingdom rather than being personally vindictive? It first involves interrogating our motives. For instance, when we are angry about a political situation, we should ask ourselves if it is because true worship is being impeded, the church is being attacked, and the gospel cannot spread? Or are we just afraid our way of life and standard of living are hindered? There are plenty of things about our culture that can provoke indignation. The question is, are they the same things that make God angry? You and I have to answer that before God.

While emphasizing a corporate concern for the kingdom, I do not want to give the impression that personal matters are never kingdom matters. The protection of your children, the defense of your character, the abuse of human rights, and the freedom to worship personally can all be matters that ultimately serve God's eternal kingdom purposes and therefore warrant imprecatory prayers. The point is to stop and ask, "Is this a matter that God is ultimately concerned about or is this only a private concern?"

How to Pray

The psalmist also spurs us to transform our anger into strategic petitions. We are not expressing personal vengeance; we are praying for God to impede attacks against the church. Those impediments can come in several ways. Most commonly, the psalmists pray that attacks on the church would come to nothing. In Psalm 129:5, the psalmist pleads that those who "hate Zion" would be shamed. Sometimes shame means embarrassment in the Bible, but in the Psalter it usually refers to disappointment. That is what it means in these psalms—that the enemy's efforts would be short-lived

Similarly, David prays in Psalm 140 that the "desires of the wicked" would not be granted (v. 8), that their plans would not "succeed" (v. 8, NIV), that "burning coals [would] fall on them," and that they would be "thrown into the fire, into miry pits, never to rise" (v. 10, NIV). This is similar to the way David prayed in Psalm 58:8 (NIV), when he asked that they be like a "slug that melts away." He was not thinking of their persons but the effectiveness of their work. Similarly, we might pray that someone's attempts to discourage a Christian's faith in the workplace would be spoiled and his influence melt away.

The psalmists then teach us to pray that enemies of the kingdom would have no esteem. One pleads in Psalm 129:8 that no blessing would come to an enemy of the church lest he be mistaken for a believer. Some enemies of the kingdom are identified by the world as representatives of it. The psalmist urges us to pray that their true colors would be made clear. In Psalm 140:11 (NIV), David calls us to implore God to prevent those who spread lies from becoming influential: "May slanderers not be established in the land; may disaster hunt down the violent." Therefore, we might pray that one who poses as a Christian while promoting an agenda hostile to God's Word would be shown for who he is and lose his good reputation.

Finally, the psalmists lead us to pray for the destruction of all of God's enemies. Usually in the Psalms, that destruction is pictured as one falling into a trap he laid for someone else. Therefore, if he slanders, his downfall will be slander. If he attacks with force, force will destroy him. It is what we call poetic justice: "[M]ay the mischief of their lips engulf them. . . . Let the wicked fall into their own nets" (Psalm 140:9; 141:10).

This theme introduces us to the most disturbing prayer in the whole Psalter, "Blessed shall he be who takes your little ones and dashes them against the rock!" (Psalm 137:8–9). First, we must understand that "Babylon," against whom this saying is directed, represents every force hostile to God. The final destruction of every Babylon is described poignantly in Revelation 18:2 and fulfills the prophecies of passages like Jeremiah 51:56 and Isaiah 13. So who then are her infants? `Ollel in Hebrew and nepios and teknon in Greek do not designate age as much as relationship. Therefore, these "children" are the followers of the evil kingdom (cf. Psalm 2:9; Jeremiah 19:11; Revelation 12:5; 19:15). So the psalmist is not praying barbarically that their infants would be beaten to death but that all who continue the efforts of hostility against God would be destroyed.

If these children are metaphorical, it is possible that the rock could be as well. Babylon was built on a flat plain, so there were no cliffs or rocks nearby. Paul said the rock was Christ (1 Corinthians 10:4). Jesus said he would be the stone upon which the opponents to his kingdom meet their demise (Matthew 21:42–44). Daniel saw the kingdom that smashed all others in the form of a stone not shaped by human hands (Daniel 2:34–35). We can pray, then, that the wicked kingdom and all its followers would be utterly destroyed by Jesus Christ.

Praying this way ensures we will be angry the right way. It ensures that the anger we feel so passionately at times will not result in rash words and actions against others. Because we have taken these things to a God who cares about justice and has promised he can and will execute justice, we can live at peace knowing we have made our petitions before God, *leaving* them in his hands.

Pray with Christ

Finally, these are prayers we pray *along with Christ*. In other words, these are his prayers that we are called to imitate. Not all evangelical authors are agreed on the present-day applicability of the imprecatory psalms. C. S. Lewis thought that they were un-Christian and that their only benefit was to show us what conspiracies do to human beings.[2] Even a great scholar like J. J. Stewart Perowne said of Psalm 109, "In the awfulness of its anathemas, the psalm surpasses everything of its kind in the Old Testament."[3] Alexander Maclaren said of Psalm 69, "It is impossible to bring such utterances into harmony with the teachings of Jesus, and the attempt to vindicate them ignores plain facts and does violence to plain words. Better far to let them stand as a monument of the earlier stage of God's progressive revelation, and discern clearly the advance which Christian ethics has made on them."[4] Bible-believing Christians can disagree on this matter, but I believe they are useful to the church, especially the anxious Christian, when prayed within the parameters I have discussed above.[5]

The final question is this: do these prayers really work? Does God really hear the prayers of his people and bring down those forces that are arrayed against them in this life? If you think through contemporary history, there are several bad guys who tormented God's people, like Nicolae Ceausescu and Slobodan Milosevic, who are now nobodies. It's not difficult to remember a few longer ago like Herod the Great, Attila the Hun, Genghis Khan, and Adolf Hitler. Andree Seu Peterson helps us remember more:

> You forgot about Haiti's "Baby Doc" Duvalier, now living on handouts in France; Ethiopia's Mengistu Haile

Mariam, under tight security in Zimbabwe; Chilean dictator General Pinochet, an old man hunted; Paraguay's General Alfredo Stroessner, hiding out in Brazil; Uganda's Idi Amin, forgotten somewhere in Saudi Arabia; Jean-Bedel Bokassa, who once crowned himself Emperor of the Central African Republic, dressed in robes and shoes of pearl, perched upon a gold-plated throne shaped like an eagle, living in a marble palace lit by chandeliers. His extravagance ruined his country and he was overthrown, and fled.[6]

Even if you could only think of one, you would have to conclude with John Calvin: "When any one crime calls forth visible manifestations of His anger, it must be because He hates all crimes; and, on the other hand, His leaving many crimes unpunished only proves that there is a judgment in reserve, when the punishment now delayed shall be inflicted."[7]

These men were "Babylons" tormenting God's people, impeding the progress of the gospel. All of these named, along with their "children," have been dashed against the Rock who remains the "King of the Ages," and he shall reign forever and ever. Give your anger to God and pray for that kingdom to come and for all others to be extinguished to the glory of God.

Questions for Reflection/Discussion

1. What is something that has made you angry recently?

2. Do you sometimes find yourself believing that all anger is sinful anger? What is the distinction between sinful anger and righteous anger?

3. How must we respond to our anger?

Prayer

Focus specifically on Psalm 140. Read through the psalm once, noticing the progression of David's prayer as he asks for deliverance and justice, maintaining a spirit of trust. Think through whatever may be causing you anger and pray this psalm in your own words, asking God to give you peace both by relieving you of your anger and by working on your behalf. Express your trust in his care for you and his power to work on your behalf. Ask God to show you constructive, God-honoring ways to address the situation.

24

He Loves You

Psalm 139

O LORD, you have searched me and known me!
(Psalm 139:1)

THE JEWISH POET Ibn Ezra (1092–1167) called Psalm 139 the "crown of all the psalms." Surely this was because every believer who meditates on it feels so thoroughly loved by God.[1] It is an appropriate place for us to end our study of the Psalms.

Throughout my life and ministry, as I have experienced times of emotional distress, anxiety, and depression and ministered to people experiencing the same, I have become convinced that there is not a problem we experience in life that cannot be solved or put into proper perspective when we believe that God loves us.

Psychologist Gary Chapman proposes that just as there are different verbal languages, there are different emotional languages.[2] Therefore, just as it is necessary to learn a foreign language in order to communicate cross-culturally, it is necessary to learn what really conveys love to another person. Chapman identifies five different ways ("languages") individuals feel loved: quality time, words of affirmation, gifts, acts of service, and physical touch. God is able to personally minister each of these to you and to me. More than that, only God is perfectly fluent in all the ways that we express love and, through them, he is able to calm every anxiety.

He Knows You (vv. 1–6)

God speaks just the right language to us because he knows us completely. Patrick Henry Reardon says, "The Psalmist could have written, very simply, 'Lord, Your knowledge of me is total.' However, instead of one verb to describe God's knowledge of the heart, the author uses six."[3] God's sovereignty overwhelms some people; it offends others. However, in this passage, God's sovereign knowledge is intended to console. There should be great relief that God understands all mysteries and we do not have to. We don't have to figure out the mysteries of life or even our own lives.

Our good God proactively searches us in order to map out the best paths for our lives. The word translated "searched" (v. 1) is used elsewhere in the Bible to describe careful investigation (cf. Jeremiah 23:23f; Psalm 44:21). Similarly, the word translated "discern" (v. 3a, NIV) is similar to a term for winnowing wheat by spreading it out so the wind can blow away the chaff.[4] God's is a thoroughgoing investigative knowledge. The present tenses of the verbs in verse 5 convey that God's scrutiny of our actions and thoughts is constant.[5]

He knows even our most basic movements: "You know when I sit and when I rise" (v. 2, NIV). Though he manages the whole universe, he knows every time we stand up or sit down. He also knows our schedules, like our "going out and [our] lying down" (v. 3, NIV). And "before a word is on [our] tongue," he "know[s] it completely" (v. 4, NIV). God also knows our thoughts. This too can be encouraging because it assures us that God is able to answer the real needs of our hearts, even if we can't shape our thoughts into intelligible prayers.

Such knowledge should be daunting to sinners. William Law said that he would rather be hanged and his body thrown in a swamp than that anyone should be allowed to look into his heart.[6] In his *Pensées*, Blaise Pascal said, "If only people could see our thoughts, we would not have four friends in the world."[7] There is no hope of making God think better of us by trying to edit our thoughts into more positive forms or putting them in a better light by gratuitous words. God knows their real nature because he knows the real nature of our hearts. You and I can fool ourselves and we can fool others, but God always knows the truth.

God's knowledge of our hearts makes verse 5 all the more astounding. God powerfully "hem[s]" or hedges us in. That word (*tsôr*) is the same used for a bag that protects a treasure (2 Kings 5:23; 12:10). A similar idea is in view here, because the next clause says, "you lay your hand upon me" (v. 5, NIV). This is the image of God putting his hand over us as one would grasp a treasured possession. Such treasuring, despite our depravity, explains the wonder of verse 6. God knows us better than we know ourselves yet loves us better than we can love ourselves. He provides ultimate affirmation because, although he knows the worst about us, he chooses to love us anyway. God has seen our thoughts and despite it all, continues to hear us and love us.

He Is with You (vv. 7–12)

David exults in God's nearness in verses 7–12. Not only does God know us; he is with us. The fact that our God pledged to be constantly with us and put flesh on that promise in Jesus distinguishes the Christian faith from all other religions. Such grace should cause us to exclaim, "What other nation is so great as to have their gods near them the way the LORD our God is near us whenever we pray to him?" (Deuteronomy 4:7).

Those who think David desperately wants to flee God's presence are mistaken. The great Old Testament scholar E. J. Young refuted those who made that false accusation.[8] It is impossible to square such an interpretation with expressions of gratitude for God's omnipresence, even his delicate attention to David in the womb, "I praise you because I am fearfully and wonderfully made" (v. 14, NIV). He is overwhelmed with gratitude for the personal, loving, and protecting presence of God. Contrasting extremes like "heavens . . . depths" and "dawn . . . far side of the sea" (vv. 8–9, NIV) are examples of a literary technique called merism. The psalmist is demonstrating that we can never get beyond God's loving attention. If he were to go to the outer reaches of space, beyond the great walls of galaxies, God would already be there. And if he were to go to the place of departed souls (Sheol) he would bump into God there, too. The gospel has intensified this reality for us. Because Jesus descended into the grave, we no longer have to be afraid of death. We are now able to say, to be there "is far better" (Philippians 1:23).

After traveling up and down in verse 8, David turns to the expanses of east and west in verses 9–10. The "wings of the morning" is the ancient expression for the pathway of the sun from east to west. There is no place on the seemingly endless circumference of the universe where David would be beyond God's attention.

Finally, David confronts an understandable fear for a person of that time, the darkness. There were no electric lights or night-vision goggles so at night he was vulnerable to attack by both human and animal intruders. However, God always views us as if we are in the broad daylight; we are never hidden from his protective sight. This truth exhorts us to live bravely! Whenever God tells his people to be courageous, he always assures them he is with them. The most familiar example is found in Joshua 1:5–9. God tells his people not to be afraid to cross the Jordan because he will be with them. God's repeated call to be "strong and [very] courageous" (vv. 6, 7, 9) is surrounded like loving arms by his promise to be with them (vv. 5, 9). Therefore, this expansive promise to be with us is intended to make us brave.

He Made You (vv. 13–18)

In the second half of the psalm, God speaks three more love languages: touch, gift-giving, and service. When I was in college,

I went to a mountain village in Haiti. When we arrived, we were greeted like dignitaries. The villagers expressed their appreciation through hugs, handshakes, and pats on the back. However, an even greater show of their appreciation and love was expressed later when the villagers brought their personal mattresses to the church for us to sleep on. Only the "wealthiest" could afford one mattress per house and they brought that one for us. Their touch and their gifts left no doubt that they loved us for our service.

God first touched us when he "created" us in our mother's wombs (v. 13, NIV). While God ceased his *de novo* creative work on the seventh day, he remains active as a craftsman. The terminology here, for instance, is similar to that used to describe the crafting of the earth (Genesis 14:19, 22). John echoes the same idea in his gospel. The Greek could be read this way: "Through [Jesus] all things were made [at the beginning of the world]; without him nothing was made that is being made" (John 1:3, NIV). In other words, Jesus is still actively involved in the crafting of every flower, every tree, every bumblebee, every butterfly, and every baby.[9] We do not believe, like deists, that God only set things in motion. We believe in God's immanence, his active involvement in our world.

The imagery gets even better in verse 14. The NIV translation depends on two interpretive choices. For one, translators inserted the word "made"; it is not in the Hebrew. Secondly, they interpret the verbal combination translated "wonderfully" in a way unnecessary. The actual verb is more naturally translated "distinguished." Therefore, the translation is more literally, "I praise you because I am distinguished." Typically, this word is used to describe the distinction that befits one who is the beneficiary of God's special covenantal love.[10] This is a theologically loaded word. David is not saying that God manipulated DNA appropriately so that we would form into human beings instead of orangutans. Rather, God uniquely touched us and set his covenant love on us the moment we were conceived. David's reflections are generic descriptions of human formation in the womb; he praises God for his particular providence toward him. His exclamation, "How precious *to me* are your thoughts" [emphasis mine], invites imitation by all believers.[11]

This is the kind of love described in Romans 9:11–13. In order to prove election was not based on works, Paul reminds us that God set his love on Jacob while he was still in Rebekah's womb. Obviously, such love long preceded any of Jacob's works— which were mostly bad anyway. This *in utero* love cures us of any delusions of works-righteousness. God loved you before you had a chance to do anything. On the other hand, if you think you have lost God's love because you have behaved poorly, this also proves you wrong. God set his love on you before the foundation of the world and marked you with distinction at conception.

God's love even preceded your conception (vv. 15–18). He set it on us while he was planning history. The expression in verse 15 (NIV) is similar to verse 13, only richer: "My frame was not hidden from you when I was made in the secret place, when I was woven together in the depths of the earth." It proves we were intricately made, like a weaver creates a complex tapestry.[12] If God paid such attention to us before we were born, how much more will he take care of us whether waking or sleeping (vv. 17–18)?

He Blesses You (vv. 19–24)

We might be tempted to think that the following verses ruin this beautiful psalm because David turns from sweet thoughts to what can seem like rabid denunciations of the ways of the wicked. But David is voicing the frustration anyone should have that someone would reject such a gracious God. David's passion reflects his love for a God who perfectly loves him. Poet Thomas Stanley (1625–1678) captured in verse the insolence of an image-bearer of God who rebels against the "feared hands" of the "Great Monarch" who tenderly crafted us:

As a learned artist thou mayst well foresee
The motions of that work is framed by thee:
Thou first into this dust a soul didst send,
Thy hand my skin did o'er my bones extend,
Which greater masterpiece, whilst I admire,
I fall down lost, in seeking to rise higher:
And finding 'bove my self, my self to be,
Turn to that nothing, from whence raised by Thee.[13]

This is the true tragedy of abortion and embryonic stem cell research; an individual known and planned before time and crafted into a human being by Jesus is redefined as the result of purely natural causes and is nothing more than an appendage on a woman's body. Tragically, human beings who have been covenantally distinguished are reduced to "stem cells," which can be bought, sold, and manipulated like garden bulbs. Abortion and embryonic research are tragedies for the babies, but even greater is the sin of rejecting a magnanimously gracious and loving God.

With God, we ought to hate their actions and oppose them, hoping that their actions would not only be stopped but that the wicked would be converted. The enemies of God are our enemies, but as those who have been undeservedly loved by God, we desire that they would be conquered by the gospel as well before he punishes them in judgment.

He Enables You (vv. 23–24)

If God had not subdued our wills and changed our thoughts, we would behave just as the wicked. David teaches us to pray by asking God to take his thoughts and spread them out before him like the farmer separates wheat from chaff before the wind. He prays for God to blow away all the chaff so that he can obey in a way that befits one who is on his way to heaven. David knows that if God does not enable him, he too will proceed toward the way of destruction.[14]

You and I need regular interrogation, correction, and huge stores of God's grace. Without them, we will walk in the way more natural for us—away from God and toward hell. The New Testament assures us that God provides everything we need for life and godliness (2 Peter 1:3). Therefore, we end just as humbly dependent upon God as we began. The passionate love of God for us demands passionate love from us. Such passionate love can only be maintained by the love of Christ, on which we must be constantly dependent. Paul assures us in Philippians that God is able to supply all of our needs according to his riches in Christ Jesus (Philippians 4:19).

I remember when my children first took notice of home movies. I was trying to organize the footage we had taken of them as infants, and they got interested. In fact, they sort of got addicted to them. They watched the same videos of themselves over and over again. Their favorite images were of birthdays and Christmas and their grandparents' house. Most often, the scene was of them as infants sitting in the middle of the living room with one gift after another being handed to them by a loving adult. By the end, you can barely see the children because they're buried in a mound of ribbons and bows and wrapping paper. The only way to find a child is when they're flitting from one present to another. There are so many that no single one can be focused on very long—there are just too many presents. Along with the gifts come lots of hugs and kisses. My kids love to watch those movies. Who wouldn't? Who wouldn't love to see himself or herself showered with gifts and shown affection?

Psalm 139 is every Christian's very own home movie. Here is a heavenly Father who understands you comprehensively, is with you unfailingly, has crafted you intentionally, gives to you generously, and serves you faithfully so that you can finish the Christian life with joy.

Conclusion

In the Psalms, Jesus shows us the pattern our lives will follow when we are united to him. We see that pattern as we hear Jesus cry out in distress through the psalmists. The Psalms reveal a Savior who never dismisses our emotions as invalid or condemns us for our lack of faith. By means of the Psalms, Jesus provides inspired vocabulary for expressing to God the full range of our emotional experience.

We see that pattern as we hear Jesus shout praises through the psalmists, thanking God for deliverance and praising him for his provision. It is the pattern Jesus explains in some of his final words to his disciples before his crucifixion: "I have told you these things, so that in me you may have peace. In this world you will have trouble. But take heart! I have overcome the world" (John 16:33, NIV). Jesus never ignores the fact that we will face many struggles in a world broken by sin, but he also never leaves us in our struggles. When our lives are united to Jesus, we can have peace because he is there with us through every step of our human experience; and we can have hope, because he stands at the end of our journey, stretching out scarred hands to receive us into his eternal joy. Truly only Jesus can enable us to say:

> You turned my wailing into dancing;
> > you removed my sackcloth and clothed me with joy,
> that my heart may sing your praises and not be silent.
> > LORD my God, I will praise you forever. (Psalm
> > 30:11–12, NIV)

Questions for Reflection/Discussion

1. Which of the five expressions of God's love for you resonate with you most?

2. Which expressions of God's love for you in this psalm were most assuring to you?

3. How does Jesus prove God's love for us?

4. What are your biggest takeaways from this study of the Psalms?

5. What psalms or particular verses were most helpful to you?

Prayer

Being convinced God loves you is perhaps the greatest key to finding peace, hope, and joy in him. Pray through the five sections of this psalm and reflect on the ways this text elaborates on God's love for you:

- God knows you (vv. 1–6).
- God is with you (vv. 7–12).
- God made you (vv. 13–18).
- God blesses you (vv. 19–24).
- God enables you (vv. 23–24).

Consider how his vast, deep love for you speaks to the specific struggles you may be facing today. Talk to God about the ways his love and intimate knowledge of you and your situation give you the strength to move forward with hope. Praise him for faithfully leading you in the way everlasting.

Endnotes

Introduction

1. John Calvin (1509–64), The Author's Preface, *Psalms 1–35*, xxxvi–xxxvii.

2. C. S. Lewis, "Sweeter Than Honey," *Reflections on the Psalms* (1958), republished within *C. S. Lewis: Selected Books* (London: HarperCollins, 2002), 310.

3. Calvin, *Psalms 1–35*, xxxvi–xxxvii.

1: The Truly Happy Person

1. W. K. Tweedie, ed., *Select Biographies* (Nabu Press, 2010), 2.259.

2. H. G. Wells, *The Fate of Man*, reprint (Riverdale, NY: Ayer Co., 1970), 247.

3. H. A. Ironside, *Studies on Book One of the Psalms* (New York: Loizeaux, 1952), 9–10.

2: I Know His Hands

1. John Newton, "Come, My Soul, Thy Suit Prepare" (1779), hymn 459, *The Lutheran Hymnal* (St. Louis: Concordia Publishing House, 1941), 459.

2. Charles Wesley, "Arise, My Soul, Arise" (1742).

3. C. H. Spurgeon, *The Treasury of David* (McLean, VA: Macdonald, 1872), 1:45–46.

4. R. Kent Hughes, *1001 Great Stories & "Quotes"* (Wheaton, IL: Tyndale House, 1998), 326–27.

5. R. Laird Harris, Gleason L. Archer, Jr., and Bruce K. Waltke, *Theological Wordbook of the Old Testament, Vol. 2* (Chicago: Moody Press, 1981), 863.

3: Deliverance from Depression

1. D. Martyn Lloyd-Jones, *Spiritual Depression* (Grand Rapids: Eerdmans, 1965).

2. Oswald Chambers, "Taking the Initiative against Depression," *My Utmost for His Highest*, February 17, https://utmost.org/taking-the-initiative-against-depression.

3. Authorities like Andrew Bonar and George Horne said that such was the consensus of the early church. They say men like Augustine, Jerome, Ambrose, Arnobius, Cassiodorus, Hilary, Prosper, and Tertullian all viewed the Psalms as the prayers of Christ.

4. Dietrich Bonhoeffer, *Psalms: The Prayer Book of the Bible*, trans. Eberhard Bethge (Minneapolis: Augsburg Press, 1970), 18–19.

5. For other examples compare, Matthew 21:13 with Psalm 118:26; John 13:18 with Psalm 41:9; Matthew 16:27 with Psalm 62:12.

6. Peter C. Craigie, *Psalms 1–50* in *Word Biblical Commentary*, vol. 19 (Waco, TX: Word Publishers, 1983), 93–94.

4: Justice for the Desperate

1. Craigie, *Psalms 1–50*, 99.

2. Charles Haddon Spurgeon, *Autobiography: The Full Harvest* (Edinburgh: Banner of Truth, 1973), 197.

3. Mitchell Dahood, *Psalms 1–50, AB* (New York: Doubleday, 1963), 40.

4. Alexander Whyte. *Lord, Teach Us to Pray* (Vancouver: Regent College, 1922/1998), 89–93.

5: The God You Can Know

1. Spurgeon, *Treasury of David*, 215.

2. Alexander Maclaren, *The Psalms: Psalms I–XXXVIII* (New York: A. C. Armstrong, 1896), 152.

3. Spurgeon, *Treasury of David*, 218-19.

4. C. S. Lewis, *The Great Divorce* (San Francisco: Harper, 1946), 90.

5. Spurgeon, *Treasury of David*, 232; Henry Ward Beecher, *Royal Truths*, reprint (Sydney Wentworth Press, 2019).

6. Anne Ross Cousin, "The Sands of Time Are Sinking," *The Hymnal* (Louisville: The General Assembly of the Presbyterian Church in the USA, 1895).

6: The Victorious Death

1. C. H. Spurgeon, "The Saddest Cry from the Cross," #2803, January 7, 1877, https://www.spurgeongems.org/vols46-48/chs2803.pdf.

2. Jonathan Kozol, *Rachel and Her Children: Homeless Families in America* (New York: Random House, 2006), 82, 85, 88.

3. This insight comes from Ironside, *Psalms*, 142.

4. Charles Wesley, "And Can It Be That I Should Gain," *Trinity Hymnal* (Suwanee, GA: Great Commission Publications, 2008), 455.

7: I Believe . . . The Lord Is My Shepherd

1. William L. Pettingill, "The Twenty-Second Psalm," *Christ in the Psalms*, reprint of 1937 edition (Scotts Valley, CA: CreateSpace, 2015).

2. J. J. Stewart Perowne, *Commentary on the Psalms*, vol. 1 (Grand Rapids: Kregel, 1989), 248.

3. Ironside, *Psalms,* 148.

4. W. Phillip Keller, *A Shepherd Looks at Psalm 23* (Grand Rapids: Zondervan, 2007).

5. F. W. Boreham, *A Temple of Topaz* (New York: Abingdon, 1928), 211.

6. Keller, *Psalm 23,* 50.

7. Keller, *Psalm 23,* 76

8. H. C. Leupold, *Exposition of Psalms* (Grand Rapids: Baker, 1977), 213.

9. Keller, *Psalm 23,* 99–109.

10. C. S. Lewis, *Mere Christianity* (New York: HarperCollins, 1952), 134.

11. John Bunyan, *The Pilgrim's Progress* in *The Complete Works of John Bunyan* (Philadelphia: Bradley, Garrettson and Co., 1872), 224.

12. Charles L. Allen, *God's Psychiatry: Healing for Your Troubled Heart* (Grand Rapids: Revell, 1953), 15.

8: Four Prayers, Four Promises

1. Spurgeon, *Treasury of David*, 1:391.

2. Ironside, *Psalms*, 157.

3. Ironside, *Psalms*, 157.

4. H. A. Ironside, *The Epistles of John and Jude* (Grand Rapids: Kregel Academic, 1949), 25.

5. Craigie, *Psalms 1–50*, 222.

6. *Westminster Confession of Faith in Modern English,* 11.5 (Orlando: Evangelical Presbyterian Church, 2017), 21.

7. Roland H. Bainton, *Here I Stand: The Life of Martin Luther* (Nashville: Abingdon, 2013), 382.

9: When Accused

1. Heiko Oberman, *Luther: Man between God and the Devil* (New Haven, CT: Yale University Press, 2006), 104.

2. Frances Havergal, "Take My Life and Let It Be," *Trinity Hymnal* (Lawrenceville, GA: Great Commission Publications, 2008), 585.

3. W. S. Danley, "All Things for Good: A Funeral Sermon," *Homiletic Review* (New York: Funk & Wagnalls, 1900), 237.

4. Dakin Andone, "They Pledge. Get Hazed. The Cycle Continues," *CNN Health*, December 8, 2018, https://www.cnn.com/2018/08/25/health/hazing-dangers-fraternities-sororities/index.html.

10: Waiting Confidently

1. Shelby Foote, *The Civil War: A Narrative*, vol. 3 (New York: Random House, 1974), 1045.

2. The article was the forerunner to his book, William Willimon, *Worship as Pastoral Care* (Nashville: Abingdon, 1982).

3. Richard Sibbes, *A Breathing After God* (Pensacola, FL: Pavlik Press, 2012), Kindle Edition, 449.

4. C. S. Lewis, *Reflections on the Psalms* (New York: Harcourt Brace, 1958), 90–98.

11: Thy Kingdom Come

1. Ironside, *Psalms*, 179–80.

2. C. I. Scofield, *Scofield Reference Bible* (London: Oxford, 1917), 599.

3. James E. Adams, *War Psalms of the Prince of Peace: Lessons from the Imprecatory Psalms* (Phillipsburg: P & R, 1991), 8.

4. Craigie, *Psalms*, 41.

5. Harry Mennega, "The Ethical Problem of the Imprecatory Psalms," master's thesis, Westminster Theological Seminary, 1959, 38.

6. George Horne, *A Commentary on the Book of Psalms in which their literal and historical sense, as they relate to King David and the people of Israel, is illustrated; and their application to the Messiah, to the church, and to individuals as members thereof* (New York: Robert Carter, 1845), 17–18. See also Andrew Bonar, *Christ and His Church in the Book of Psalms* (New York: Robert Carter, 1860), ix.

7. Horne, *A Commentary on the Book of Psalms*, 27–28.

8. Adams, *War Psalms of the Prince of Peace*, 25.

9. Geoffrey Wainwright, *Doxology: The Praise of God in Worship, Doctrine, and Life* (New York: Oxford, 1980), 434.

12: When Life Gets to You

1. Nicholas Wolterstorff, *Until Justice and Peace Embrace* (Grand Rapids, MI: Eerdmans, 1983), 9.

2. Cornelius Plantinga, *Engaging God's World: A Christian Vision of Faith, Learning, and Living* (Grand Rapids, MI: Eerdmans, 2002), 96–97.

3. Arthur Tappan Pierson, *George Müller of Bristol* (London: James Nisbet & Co., 1899), 183.

4. Ironside, *Psalms*, 218.

13: Life under Heaven

1. *Conversations with Luther: Selections from Recently Published Portions of Table Talk*, ed./trans. Preserved Smith and Herbert Percival Gallinger (Boston: The Pilgrim Press, 1915), 95.

2. Carl Friedrich Keil and Franz Delitzsch, *Commentary on the Old Testament*, Vol. 5 (Peabody, MA: Hendrickson, 1996), 349–50.

3. Gordon Franz, "Archaeology, Assyrian Reliefs & the Psalms of the Sons of Korah," *Bible and Spade* 20, no. 1 (Winter 2007), 13–14.

4. Charles Colson, *The Body* (Dallas: Word, 1992), 238.

5. John White, *The Golden Cow: Materialism in the Twentieth-Century Church* (Downers Grove, IL: IVP, 1979), 47, 54.

6. John Wesley, "The Use of Money," *The Works of John Wesley*, vol. 6 (London: Wesleyan Conference Office, 1872), 133.

7. White, *The Golden Cow*, 38–39.

8. White, *The Golden Cow*, 57–58.

9. Nathaniel Hawthorne, *The Golden Touch* (New York: St. Martin's Press, 1992).

14: Pardon for Sin and a Peace That Endures

1. *Westminster Confession of Faith in Modern English*, 5.5.

2. *Westminster Confession of Faith in Modern English*, 11.5.

15: The Light of Life

1. Isobel S. Kuhn, *Green Leaf in Drought Time* (Chicago: Moody Press, 1957).

2. Derek Kidner, *Psalms 1–72* (Leister, England: Inter-Varsity Press, 1973), 202.

3. Trevor Lummis, *Pitcairn Island: Life and Death in Eden* (Brookfield, VT: Ashgate Publishing, 1997).

16: Surviving a Surprise Attack

1. John Calvin, *Commentary on the Book of Psalms*, vol. 2 (Grand Rapids, MI: Baker, 1981), 445.

2. Charles Haddon Spurgeon, *The Treasury of David*, vol. 3 (London: Passmore & Alabaster, 1872), 153.

3. Leupold, *Exposition of the Psalms*, 470.

4. William J. Peterson and Ardythe E. Peterson, *The Complete Book of Hymns* (Carol Stream, IL: Tyndale House, 2006), 405.

17: Backward Praise

1. Sinclair B. Ferguson, "Ordo Salutis," *New Dictionary of Theology* (Downers Grove, IL: IVP Academic, 1988), 480.

2. Isaac Watts, "How Sweet and Awesome Is the Place," *Hymns and Sacred Songs,* 1707.

3. See Walter C. Kaiser, Jr., *Toward Rediscovering the Old Testament* (Grand Rapids, MI: Zondervan, 1987), 64.

4. David B. Calhoun, "'His Bright Designs': The Doctrine of Providence," *Presbyterion* 24 (Spring 1998): 3–8.

5. William Barker, "Reflections on Church History from a Recent Reading of Jonathan Edwards's *A History of the Work of Redemption*," in *Faithful Ministry: An Ecclesial Festschrift in Honor of the Rev. Dr. Robert S. Rayburn,* ed. Max Rogland (Eugene, OR: Wipf & Stock, 2019), 9–12.

6. Jonathan Edwards, *A History of the Work of Redemption: An Outline of Church History* (New York: American Tract Society, 1850), 430.

7. Leupold, *Exposition of the Psalms,* 477.

8. On this see *Westminster Confession of Faith in Modern English*, 3.1.

9. Norman Wirzba, *Food and Faith: A Theology of Eating* (Cambridge: Cambridge University Press, 2011), 63.

10. While the examples occur in Books 1 and 2, his conclusion occurs in 7.17.23. Augustine, *Confessions* (New York: Liveright Publishing, 1943), 154.

11. Hughes, *1001 Great Stories and Quotes*, 92.

18: Come and See What God Has Done

1. Marvin Tate, *Psalms 51–100.* Word Biblical Commentary, vol. 20 (Dallas: Thomas Nelson, 1991), 151.

2. Lewis, *Reflections on the Psalms,* 95.

3. John Calvin, *Institutes of the Christian Religion* (Grand Rapids, MI: Wm. B. Eerdmans, 1995), 2.15.4, 3.8.2.

4. Calvin, *Institutes*, 3.8.5.

5. Calvin, *Institutes*, 3.8.6

6. John Calvin, *Commentaries on the Epistles of Paul to the Galatians and Ephesians* (Grand Rapids, MI: Baker House, 1979), 187.

7. Quoted in Spurgeon, *Treasury of David*, 126.

19: The Church Is for Weaklings and Nobodies

1. See Rowland E. Prothero, *The Psalms in Human Life* (New York: E. P. Dutton, 1908), 22, 71, 119, 182–213, 258, 358.

2. Bruce M. Metzger, *A Textual Commentary on the Greek New Testament* (Stuttgart: United Bible Societies, 1971), 724.

3. On this see Paul Copan, *A Moral Monster? Making Sense of the Old Testament God* (Grand Rapids: Baker, 2011), 159-161.

20: The Church Made Strong

1. Vince Bantu, "Multiethnic Roots of Christianity Part III: Early African Christianity." (November 15, 2016), http://www.jude3project.com/blog/ethopia. See also Bantu, "Egyptian Ethnic Identity Development in Anti-Chalcedonian Coptic Literature," PhD diss., The Catholic University of America, Washington, DC, 2015.

2. Philip Jenkins, "Believing in the Global South," *First Things*, December 2006, https://www.firstthings.com/article/2006/12/believing-in-the-global-south.

3. Kidner, *Psalms 1–72*, 243.

4. Johann Christoff Arnold, *Drained: Stories of People Who Wanted More* (Walden, NY: Plough Publishing, 2011), 52.

5. Franz Delitzsch, *Psalms,* vol. 5, Commentary on the Old Testament in Ten Volumes (Grand Rapids, MI: Eerdmans, 1986), 263.

6. See Acts 4:4; 5:14; 6:1, 7; 9:31, 35, 42; 11:21, 24; 14:1, 21; 16:5; 17:12.

7. On this see John Murray, *Romans: Volume 2* in *New International Commentary on the New Testament,* (Grand Rapids, MI: Eerdmans, 1965), 91–96.

8. Jonathan Edwards, *The Works of Jonathan Edwards* (New Haven, CT: Yale University Press, 1977), 135. See also Iain Murray, *The Puritan Hope* (Edinburgh: Banner of Truth, 2014), 175–8.

9. Charles Simeon, *Horae Homileticae Vol. 9: Jeremiah to Daniel* (London: Holdsworth and Ball, 1832), 474.

10. John Bunyan, *The Works of John Bunyan*, ed. George Offor, vol. 1 (New York: Frederick A. Stokes, 1920), 19.

21: Life under the Cross

1. Bonar, *Christ and His Church in the Book of Psalms*, ix.

2. Augustine, *Exposition of the Book of Psalms*, ed. Philip Schaff (New York: Christian Literature Publishing, 1886), 218.

3. Calvin, *Institutes*, 3.8.1.

4. William S. Plummer, *Psalms* (Edinburgh: Banner of Truth, 1978), 690.

5. Charles H. Spurgeon, *Selected Works of Charles Spurgeon*, vol. 3 (Raleigh, NC: LuLu Press, 2003), digital, chapter 6.

6. Dan Allender and Tremper Longman III, *Bold Love* (Colorado Springs: NavPress, 1992), 252–254.

7. On this see Mary Potter Engel, *John Calvin's Perspectival Anthropology* (Eugene, OR: Wipf & Stock, 2002), 170–173.

8. Joseph M. Stowell, *Strength for the Journey: Day by Day with Jesus* (Chicago: Moody Press, 2002), 165.

22: The Real World

1. Edmund P. Clowney, *The Message of 1 Peter*, The Bible Speaks Today (Downers Grove, IL: IVP Academic, 1989), 15.

2. Matthew Henry, *Matthew Henry's Commentary on the Whole Bible*, (Peabody, MA: Hendrickson, 2009), 503.

3. Elizabeth Fox-Genovese, "A Conversion Story," *First Things* 102 (April 2000): 39–43.

4. Fox-Genovese, "A Conversion Story," 39–43.

23: What to Do with Anger

1. Keil and Delitzsch, *Commentary on the Old Testament*, Vol. 5, 800.

2. Lewis, *Reflections on the Psalms*, 20–33.

3. J. J. Stewart Perowne, *Psalms: A New Translation* (London: George Bell & Sons, 1882), 285.

4. Alexander Maclaren, *Psalms*, Vol. 2:39–89 (Hodder & Stoughton, 1893), 303.

5. On this see Cal Beisner, *Psalms of Promise: Celebrating the Majesty and Faithfulness of God* (Phillipsburg, NJ: Presbyterian &

Reformed, 1994), 165–185; James Montgomery Boice, *Psalms,* vol. 3 (Grand Rapids, MI: Baker, 1998), 885–886.

6. Andrée Seu Peterson, "Valley of the Gods," *World* (November 11, 2000): 28.

7. Calvin, *Institutes,* 1.5.7.

24: He Loves You

1. J. J. Stewart Perowne, *The Book of Psalms* (Grand Rapids: Kregel, 1989), 438.

2. Gary Chapman, *The 5 Love Languages: The Secret to Love That Lasts* (Chicago: Northfield Publishing, 2010).

3. Patrick Henry Reardon, *Christ in the Psalms* (Ben Lomond, CA: Conciliar Press, 2000), 277.

4. Keil and Delitzsch, *Commentary on the Old Testament,* 346.

5. Keil and Delitzsch, *Commentary on the Old Testament,* 345.

6. Robert S. Rayburn, "Above All Else the Heart," sermon on Matthew 15:1–20, December 26, 2004, http://www.faithtacoma.org/matthew/above-all-else-the-heart.

7. Blaise Pascal, *Pensees* (New York: Penguin, 1996), 8.42.

8. E. J. Young, *The Way Everlasting: A Study in Psalm 139* (Edinburgh: Banner of Truth, 1965), 45.

9. Leon Morris, *The Gospel according to John* (Grand Rapids, MI: Wm. B. Eerdmans, 1971), 80.

10. C. John Collins, "Fearfully and Wonderfully Made," *Presbyterion* 25:2 (1999): 115–120.

11. Joseph Bryant Rotherham, *Studies in the Psalms* (London: H.R. Allenson, J. George Rotherham, 1911), 566.

12. Albert Barnes, *Notes on the Bible: Psalms,* 139 (Grand Rapids, MI: Baker, 1884–85/1996).

13. Robert Atwan and Laurance Wieder, eds. *Chapters into Verse* (Oxford: Oxford University Press, 2000), 170.

14. Keil and Delitzsch, *Commentary on the Old Testament,* 354.